Machine Learning for Diabetes and Blood Glucose Prediction

Barbosa

TABLE OF CONTENTS

List of Figures

List of Tables

List of Abbreviations

Abbreviations	Full Form
AB	AdaBoost
AI	Artificial Intelligence
ANN	Artificial Neural Network
ARIMA	Autoregressive Integrated Moving Average
AUC	Area Under the Curve
BGL	Blood Glucose Level
BLE	Bluetooth Low Energy
BMI	Body Mass Index
BP	Blood Pressure
CEGA	Clarke Error Grid Analysis
CGM	Continuous Glucose Monitor/Monitoring
CNN	Convolutional Neural Network
DL	Deep Learning
DLSTM	Deep Long Short-Term Memory
DT	Decision Tree
ECG	Electrocardiogram
EDA	Exploratory Data Analysis
EGA	Error Grid Analysis
EHR	Electronic Health Records
FPGA	Field-Programmable Gate Array
GBC	Gradient Boosting Classifier
GDM	Gestational Diabetes Mellitus
GRU	Gated Recurrent Unit
HR	Heart Rate
HbA1c	Haemoglobin A1c
IoT	Internet of Things
KNN	K-Nearest Neighbours
LASSO	Least Absolute Shrinkage and Selection Operator
LDA	Linear Discriminant Analysis
LSTM	Long Short-Term Memory
LiR	Linear Regression
LightGBM	Light Gradient Boosting Machine
LoR	Logistic Regression
MAE	Mean Absolute Error
MAPE	Mean Absolute Percentage Error
MARD	Mean Absolute Relative Difference
ML	Machine Learning
MLP	Multi-Layer Perceptron

MSE	Mean Squared Error
NB	Naive Bayes
NIDDK	National Institute of Diabetes and Digestive and Kidney Diseases
NIR	Near-Infrared
NN	Neural Network
PCA	Principal Component Analysis
PH	Prediction Horizon
REGA	Rate Error Grid Analysis
RF	Random Forest
RMSE	Root Mean Square Error
RNN	Recurrent Neural Network
ROC	Receiver Operating Characteristic
ReLU	Rectified Linear Unit
SMBG	Self-Monitoring of Blood Glucose
SMO	Sequential Minimal Optimization
SMOTE	Synthetic Minority Oversampling Technique
SVM	Support Vector Machine
SVR	Support Vector Regression
T1D	Type 1 Diabetes
T2D	Type 2 Diabetes
TCN	Temporal Convolutional Network
WD	Weibull Distribution
XGBoost	Extreme Gradient Boosting

CHAPTER 1
INTRODUCTION

1.1 Overview

Diabetes mellitus, often called diabetes, has ballooned into an epidemic. Diagnosis is on the rise now, representing 90-95% of all diabetes cases, and the trend shows no sign of slowing. This surge places a burden on health-care systems. According to the International Diabetes Federation (2022), the prevalence of diabetes has reached alarming levels, with projections suggesting that by 2045, nearly 783 million adults worldwide will be affected [1].

Various ML techniques and DL algorithms have been applied in diabetes prediction. Frequently used ML and DL algorithms are NB, RF, SVM, DT, J48, Sequential Minimal Optimization (SMO), ANN (Artificial Neural Network), Multi-Layer Perceptron (MLP), Recurrent Neural Network (RNN), CNN and LSTM . Although deep research in diabetes mellitus has provided strong proficiency to classify data, there is still much to be discovered by considering the patient's diet, medication, activity, and biological, environmental, behavioral, and decision factors. Traditional ML models are easy to interpret but achieve less predictive accuracy while ensemble models provide higher accuracy. Existing studies proved that DL models performed comparatively better on complex datasets than the ML models. As reported in selected studies the accuracy achieved so far is not more than 95% by a combined model designed using the CNN-LSTM technique.

Diabetes technology refers to the hardware, devices, and software used by people with anti-diabetic medications to control diabetes and prevent complications of diabetes, to overcome the load of having diabetics, and to improve the standard of life. Several continuous glucose monitoring technologies, such as CGM and Self-Monitoring of Blood Glucose (SMBG), glucose devices, CGM with automatically controlled insulin delivery, glucose measuring technologies, and mobile devices recording and displaying ongoing trends. But CGM sensors need to be replaced every 10 to 90 days depending upon the CGM system provider. By combining data from multiple patients, trends can be found between people and general patterns can be identified.

By considering the above major concerns, technology trends, and the needs of society we designed and developed a model that predicts diabetes, creates clusters based on BGLs, simulates BGL predictions, and also predicts consequences of diabetes.
This research work aims to:

- Comparative Analysis of ML Algorithms for Diabetes Prediction
- Prediction of Diabetes using Ensemble Models
- Prediction of Blood Glucose Levels

Each part focused on multiple experimental strategies, including comparative analysis, ensemble learning, and data augmentation to enhance accuracy and generalization.

1.2 Background of Diabetes Mellitus

Diabetes is a condition where the body either fails to produce sufficient insulin or does not respond properly to it, leading to variations in BGLs. Under normal conditions, carbohydrates are broken down into glucose, which enters the bloodstream and triggers the pancreas to secrete insulin. Insulin enables cells to absorb glucose for energy or store it as glycogen in the liver and muscles. When blood glucose decreases, glucagon is secreted to convert glycogen back into glucose, maintaining energy balance.

1.2.1 Types and Causes of Diabetes

Diabetes results primarily from problems related to insulin production or utilization. The American Diabetes Association classifies the disease into three major types: Type 1 Diabetes, Type 2 Diabetes, and gestational diabetes.

Type 1 Diabetes (T1D): An autoimmune disorder in which the immune system attacks and destroys the insulin-producing beta cells, resulting in total absence of insulin. It usually begins in childhood or adolescence and requires lifelong insulin treatment.

Type 2 Diabetes (T2D): About 95% of adult occurrences of diabetes are type 2 diabetes (T2D). It occurs when the body either doesn't make enough insulin or the cells start to resist it. The main causes include obesity, poor nutrition, and inactivity.

Gestational Diabetes (GDM): Occurs in pregnancy because of hormonal imbalance, which leads to insulin resistance. It affects up to 10% of pregnancies and must be managed to prevent hurdles for both mother and child.

1.2.2 Risk Factors

The risk of developing diabetes depends on various lifestyle, genetic, and environmental factors. Below mentioned risk factors provide the foundation variables for feature engineering, where these raw attributes are transformed, selected, and optimized to improve the predictive performance of machine learning models.

Insulin Resistance: The body's reduced ability to use insulin effectively, causing fluctuations in BGL.
Family History: Genetic predisposition increases the risk of developing diabetes.
High Cholesterol: Both conditions raise the risk of heart disease and diabetic complications.
Obesity and Waist Size: Excess body fat, especially around the abdomen, is a major factor in insulin resistance.
Body Mass Index (BMI): A high BMI is directly linked to increased diabetes risk.
Age: The likelihood of diabetes increases after the age of 35.
Diet and Inactivity: High intake of processed foods and lack of physical activity significantly elevate risk levels.
Pregnancy: Hormonal changes in pregnancy can cause temporary insulin resistance.
Sleep and Stress: Poor sleep quality and psychological stress are linked to impaired glucose metabolism.
Smoking and Alcohol: Smoking increases the risk of diabetes, while moderate alcohol consumption may have a protective effect.

1.2.3 Diabetes Complications

If diabetes is not treated properly, diabetes can result in serious health complications and premature death. It can lead to cardiovascular diseases, kidney failure, stroke, nerve damage, vision loss, and other disorders. Complications are generally classified into:

Microvascular: Damage to small blood vessels causing retinopathy, nephropathy, and neuropathy.

Macrovascular: Damage to larger arteries, leading to cardiovascular diseases, leading to heart attack and stroke.

According to the World Health Organization, global prevalence of diabetes has been gradually increasing; this leads to a serious public health challenge. Long-term diabetes may cause over time serious damage to major body organs.

Maintaining BGLs within a narrow range is crucial for people with diabetes, as excessively high levels (hyperglycemia) can lead to serious long-term complications such as kidney failure and blindness, while very low levels can cause blackouts, seizures, and even death.

Diabetics take care of their BGL and how their actions influence it by taking into account many factors including meal intake, physical movements, and medicine dosage. The present aim is to build predictive models for the prediction of diabetes and the forecast of its BGL using ML and DL techniques. The system has two major components, namely, diabetes prediction and blood glucose prediction. Each of these components explores multiple modeling strategies, including comparative analysis, ensemble learning, and data augmentation, for enhancing accuracy and generalization.

Thus, by accurately predicting future glucose level variability, patients and healthcare providers can take necessary steps to prevent critical threshold levels from being reached. Predictive modeling has today become an important feature in all digital health systems and personalized medicine.

1.3 Research Motivation

While predictive modeling in healthcare is an ever-growing field, fast and generalizable models applicable to diabetes and glucose prediction remain a challenge. The usual temporal and nonlinear nature of physiological data often evades traditional statistical methods. ML models, though effective, are sometimes limited in adaptability and scalability across different patient populations.

In addition, DL algorithms can only work well when the datasets are big and diverse. In medical domains, data is often limited due to privacy concerns and the immense cost related to collecting clinical data. This calls for data augmentation methods in order to enhance the robustness and generalization of the models.

Another important motivation is the integration of various models via ensemble learning, which has been shown to improve predictive performance by combining the strengths of different algorithms. Ensemble methods, combined with complementary classical ML, DL, and data augmentation, provide a holistic approach toward achieving an optimal, accurate, and stable predictive outcome.

Some of the motivating factors towards this research include:

Early intervention: The rise in diabetic cases in the world indicates that early detection of the disease and its prevention are vital.

Use of Technology: ML and AI are making trends in healthcare, especially when it comes to predicting and diagnosing diseases.

Lower risk of developing diabetes: Personalization of strategies for the prevention and treatment of diabetes through the identification of high-risk individuals followed by targeted interventions.

Reduced healthcare costs: Catching diabetes early doesn't just help people avoid complications; it saves a lot of money for both individuals and the entire healthcare system. The earlier we spot it, the less everyone spends on treatment down the line.

Better management of diabetes: Precise prediction of fluctuations in blood glucose can lead to better management of the disease. Anticipation of changes allows patients to manage their intake of insulin, diet, and exercise much more effectively towards maintaining healthy BGL.

1.4 Problem Statement

The sharp rise in diabetes cases has become a major global health issue. The age-adjusted mortality rate associated with diabetes continues to climb each day. Early diagnosis, prevention, and control of diabetes-related complications are vital to reduce its impact on individuals and society. However, current prediction methods are often unreliable and may overlook people at high risk. Although significant advancements have been made in diabetes research, two major challenges continue to hinder progress in predictive modeling:

1. Early and Accurate Prediction of Diabetes Onset: Traditional diagnostic approaches largely rely on clinical measures such as fasting blood glucose and HbA1c levels. These fixed parameters often fail to represent complex multivariate interactions and temporal changes, making early detection a persistent challenge in preventive healthcare.

2. Reliable Prediction of BGLs in Type 1 Diabetes: In Type 1 Diabetes (T1D), BGLs vary dynamically due to multiple behavioral, physiological, and environmental

influences, including diet, physical activity, and insulin administration. Many existing prediction models struggle to effectively capture these rapid temporal shifts using a very small number of samples, particularly in short-term forecasting windows of 30, 60, and 90 minutes.

Additionally, fluctuations in glucose levels are closely linked to long-term diabetes-related complications. Predicting these complications in conjunction with glucose levels could enhance personalized disease management, yet this area remains relatively underexplored. Based on the discussed problems problem statement is defined as:

"Developing an unified framework using machine learning and ensemble models for prediction of diabetes with hybrid deep learning architectures for precise, time-series blood glucose level prediction and aid in early disease detection and prevention."

1.5 Scope of the Research

The scope of this study is to advance diabetes control and risk estimation by an evidence-based, comprehensive process. This research would not only extend as far as a basic diagnosis model and encompasses the complete data capture to the clinical risk assessment cycle.

Data Engineering and Preprocessing: This work aims to develop an efficient data pipeline for collecting, cleaning, integrating, and transforming multisensor diabetic patient data. It also involves investigating novel approaches for data augmentation in order to alleviate data sparsity and improve generalizability.

Development of Comparative Models for Glucose Forecasting: This study will comparatively develop, validate, and contrast conventional ensemble ML and new state-of-the-art DL models to determine how they fare in short-term glucose forecasting.

Feature Importance Analysis: It will examine and quantify the most influential features of the multi-sensor data, ranking those that have the maximum contribution toward the fluctuation in glucose, which could provide clinical insight into factors leading to blood sugar variation.

Patient-Centered Analysis of Data: The application involves the development of glucose data analysis and visualization techniques for individual patients that provide personalized insight to support personalized clinical decision-making.

Long-term complication prediction: The research will develop a state-of-the-art predictive model that can investigate and foresee the likelihood of a patient developing diabetes-related complications, thereby making a shift in treatment from reactive to proactive and preventive.

1.6 Significance of the study

Prediction of BGLs is important not only for diabetic patients but also for the healthcare system as a whole. Here's a breakdown of its importance:

Empowerment and self-governance: The patient can make informed decisions on food intake, exercise, and medication based on the predicted blood sugar trends.

Reduced risk of complications: The early detection of potential highs and lows will thus allow for timely intervention to avoid dangerous situations, such as hypoglycemia or hyperglycemia.

Management of Diabetes: A framework for the prediction of diabetes; therefore, integrated computational intelligence methods can enhance the accuracy of such predictions. The resulting outcome can be earlier disease detection and better management of the disease. Ultimately reducing the disease burden on individuals and society, and reducing healthcare expenditure resulting from the management of diabetes.

1.7 Research Contributions

Designing a model for predicting BGL offers significant contributions to society, doctors, and diabetic patients. These models, often leveraging ML and CGM data, empower individuals and healthcare providers with proactive insights, leading to improved health outcomes and a better quality of life.

1. This research enables the early prediction of BGL fluctuations, allowing for timely interventions to prevent critical conditions like severe hypoglycemia. It enhances patient safety and supports real-time self-management.
2. Conducted a comprehensive comparative evaluation of six ML classifiers across three benchmark diabetes datasets.
3. Developed and systematically assessed ensemble-based prediction strategies (soft voting, hard voting, and hybrid ensembles), demonstrating improved diagnostic reliability and performance compared to individual classifiers.
4. Designed a data augmentation pipeline for CGM signals, incorporating baseline drift, amplitude scaling, circadian variation, meal timing jitter, noise injection, and postprandial response variability. This approach expanded the dataset from 9 to over 426 synthetic patient profiles, enhancing model generalizability.
5. Constructed a multi-stage DL framework for glucose forecasting, integrating both univariate and multivariate prediction tasks. Hybrid architectures including DLSTM, LSTM–GRU, CNN–LSTM, and CNN–GRU were implemented and rigorously evaluated.
6. Integrated multimodal physiological signals (CGM, heart rate, breathing rate, activity, posture, acceleration, temperature, and insulin dosing) to strengthen

prediction robustness across datasets of varying sizes (20, 54, 100, and 500 patients).

7. Achieved state-of-the-art glucose prediction performance, with RMSE ≈ 2.16 mg/dL and MARD ≈ 1.02%, using a CNN–LSTM hybrid model. This performance significantly surpassed previously reported results in the literature.
8. Performed a comparative validation against prior studies, confirming that the proposed framework consistently achieved lower prediction error even when applied to higher-dimensional input spaces.
9. Proposed a unified framework that integrates diabetes prediction, glucose forecasting with its consequences for better management of diabetes.

The contribution of the thesis looks significant as it not only evaluates ML and ensemble classifiers for diabetes prediction but also proposes a unified framework combining diagnosis, glucose forecasting, clustering, and complication prediction. The integration of multimodal wearable data, synthetic augmentation techniques, and advanced DL models enhances the novelty and practical impact of the work.

1.8 Thesis Organization

The remainder of the thesis structure is outlined below:

Chapter 2 – Literature Review

This chapter provides a comprehensive survey of prior work in diabetes prediction, glucose forecasting, and ensemble learning methodologies. It synthesizes key contributions, identifies prevailing methodological approaches, and highlights unresolved challenges that form the basis for the present study.

Chapter 3 – Datasets

In this chapter the detailed characteristics of the datasets required for diabetes predictions and dataset for blood glucose prediction are presented. Three datasets namely pima, Neha Tigga Dataset and Diabetes Dataset used for Diabetes Prediction, whereas D1NAMO diabetes used for predicting blood glucose levels.

Chapter 4 – Technology for Diabetes Prediction and Blood Glucose Level Prediction

The ML and ensemble approaches for diabetes prediction and the DL algorithms used for predicting blood glucose levels are discussed in this chapter.

Chapter 5 – Experimental Setup

Three research models discussed here.

The first module presented in this chapter, details the datasets employed, preprocessing techniques applied, and the experimental framework for evaluating six ML classifiers for diabetes prediction.

The second module in this chapter outlines the dataset preprocessing pipeline, ensemble configurations (soft voting, hard voting, and hybrid ensembles), and the model training procedures for prediction of diabetes.

The third module encompasses the dataset preparation, augmentation strategies for D1NAMO dataset, and the design of hybrid DL architectures (DLSTM, LSTM–GRU, CNN–LSTM, and CNN–GRU) for forecasting blood glucose levels and predicting likelihood diabetes complications.

Chapter 6 – Results and Discussion

Experimental outcome results are reported and analyzed against conventional classifiers and related research to demonstrate the advantages of ML classifiers and ensemble-based approaches. A multi-stage experimental evaluation is conducted, and results are compared with existing DL approaches to assess forecasting accuracy and robustness.

Chapter 7 – Conclusion and Future Scope

The final chapter consolidates the principal contributions and findings of the study. It discusses limitations encountered during the research and proposes directions for future work, particularly in advancing predictive modeling and clinical applicability of diabetes diagnosis and glucose forecasting systems.

Appendix

Relevant publications are listed in Appendix A, patents in Appendix B, plagiarism reports in Appendix C.

CHAPTER 2
LITERATURE REVIEW

This chapter provides a review of existing studies focused on (1) diabetes prediction through ML and DL, (2) glucose forecasting using DL and hybrid techniques, (3) data augmentation for physiological time-series prediction, and (4) approaches for interpretability and feature relevance in medical systems. It also highlights current research limitations that informed the design of the proposed Hybrid DL Framework.

Over the last two decades, research in diabetes prediction and blood glucose forecasting has progressed by leaps and bounds. The adoption of data-driven and computational methods has significantly reshaped traditional conceptions and analysis related to diabetes progression and glucose patterns. But conventional diagnostic tools are the standard yet lacking in flexibility to adapt in real time to individual variations (World Health Organization, 2023) [2].

ML provides computers with self-learning capability from experience and does not require explicit programming. Several studies have been conducted to compare LoR, Decision Tree (DT), Support Vector Machine (SVM), Logistic Regression (LoR), K-Nearest Neighbor (KNN), Random Forest (RF), Naive Bayes (NB), and J48 algorithms in optimizing a predictive model. DL, which is a subset of ML, uses Neural Network NNs, modeling the human brain functionality, where data can be represented hierarchically to improve the quality of prediction. By embedding human-like reasoning into machines using algorithms, Artificial Intelligence (AI) is changing many aspects pertaining to human life. Specifically, in healthcare, AI -driven predictive analytics is transforming data to insights for future event prediction [3]. Some of the pivoting tools in medical AI are ML and DL, which, through technological development, help build smart systems for prediction and diagnosis of diabetes. Consequently, most current research seems to employ these methods individually or integrated in hybrid models to improve diabetes prediction. Moreover, integrated approaches using data mining and machine learning (ML) uncover hidden data patterns beyond the capabilities of analytical methods commonly used [4]; this is important in diabetes prediction.

2.1 Review on Diabetes Prediction

The latest advances in ML technologies help find hidden patterns and diagnose diabetes much earlier. Today, healthcare organizations collect huge amounts of data. But despite this wealth of information, we still struggle to truly understand it all. Extracting useful knowledge that can help us diagnose and predict diseases remains a major challenge.

Prabhu and Selvabharathi [5] employed a deep network model to predict diabetes on a pima dataset. Three stages were used by the authors to build the model: min-max normalization for data preprocessing, network model construction, and NN-FF classification for fine-tuning the test dataset to eliminate any bias. Lastly, the authors used MATLAB to complete all of the model's simulation and implementation. The authors found the best performance metric when compared to the others, reporting an F1 score of 0.808.

Jobeda Jamal Khanam et al. [6] applied seven ML algorithms on the pima dataset for predicting diabetes. The obtained result shows that the combinational model of LR with SVM performed better on diabetes prediction. The neural network with two hidden layers achieved an accuracy of 88.6%. Another review by Hussain and Naaz [7] presented an analysis of ML models on diabetes prediction between 2010 and 2019, comparing traditional ML supervised techniques against NN-based methods in terms of accuracy and efficiency.

Neha PrernaTiggaa et al. [8] performed work by comparing six ML classification methods namely LR, K-Nearest Neighbour (KNN), SVM, NB and DT and RF on the dataset of 952 participants collected through online and offline questionnaires consisting of 18 questions of diabetes and PID dataset. The experimental results demonstrate that the RF achieved the highest accuracy of 94.10% , outperforming all other models tested.

Talha et al. [9] examined diabetes risk through multivariate analysis, applying Principal component Analysis (PCA) for dimensionality reduction. Their Apriori algorithm identified body mass index and glucose levels as strongly associated factors. Comparison of neural networks (75.7% accuracy), random forests (RF), and K-means clustering indicated neural networks performed most effectively for clinical prediction tasks.

Han Wu [10] designed a model using data mining techniques to predict T2M. The implemented approach combines the K-means clustering algorithm with the LoR algorithm. They utilized the Waikato Environment Analysis on the PID dataset. Compared to the existing model, their model attained a 3.04% increase in prediction accuracy.

Ali Mohebbi et al. [11] compared logistic regression (LoR), multilayer perceptrons, and CNNs for Type 2 diabetes prediction using continuous glucose monitoring data, with CNNs performing best at 77.50% accuracy.

Diabetes prediction using ML involves training a model on a dataset of patient medical information to predict the likelihood of a person having diabetes. Nitesh Pradhana et al. [12] presented the state of art in the arena of diabetes prediction using the PID dataset. They identified difficulties in existing methods and they proposed effective solutions by using artificial neural networks (ANN) for detecting diabetes.

The proposed work achieved sufficient accuracy, with a score of 85.09%. This demonstrates the effectiveness of their approach.

Ismail et al. [13] examined 35 different ML techniques with respect to T2DM prediction. Nine feature selection algorithms were applied on three real-life diabetes datasets, and the performance comparison was performed among subjects with and without diabetes in order to understand the effectiveness of each technique in identifying those at risk.

A predictive model developed on CNN, LSTM, and ensemble methods was proposed by Swapna G. et al. [14]. This predictive model analyzed the HRV data for identifying intricate chronological patterns in the data. Then, using the identified characteristics of the data, SVM classified it accordingly.

If a patient with diabetes has an early warning system for predicting blood glucose (BG) level changes within the next half hour, they can take proactive steps to prevent spikes. For this Hrushikesh N. Mhaskar et al. [15] made a significant contribution by creating a DL model that can predict patient glucose levels 30 minutes in advance. This tool allows patients to take precautionary steps to manage their blood sugar and avoid potential complications.

Lastly, Rghioui et al. [16] developed an intelligent diagnosis system based on patient information and ML, testing algorithms such as Naive Bayes (NB), J48, ZeroR, and OneR, and finding that the Sequential Minimal Optimization (SMO) algorithm yielded the highest results.

The detailed review on recent studies performed by researchers in the field of prediction of diabetes is presented in table 2.1. It highlights the dataset used, preprocessing techniques applied, and methods or algorithms used, along with results and findings.

Table 2.1. Summary of review in Diabetes Prediction

Sr. No	Author	Dataset	Pre-processing Techniques	Methods /algorithms	Results	Findings
1	Jobeda Jamal Khanam (2021) [5]	Pima	Missing value and outlier replacement, Pearson' s correlation	DT, KNN, RF, NB, AB, LR, SVM, NN	NN with 2 hidden layers and 400 epochs got 88.6% accuracy	The authors used rarely used classifiers and recommended using and enhancing them by developing combined models.
2	Umair Muneer Butt et al. (2021) [17]	Pima	Cleaning, integration, transformation, reduction, and discretization	RF, MLP, LR Moving averages, LSTM, LiR	MLP 86.6% Precision, 85.1% Recall, and 86.083% accuracy and diabetes prediction using LSTM 87.26% accuracy	proposed a Hypothetical IoT- Based Diabetic Monitoring System
3	Eric Adua, Emman et al. (2021) [18]	private data	Expectation maximization is used to compute for the missing data	KNN,SVM, NB and DT	NB with AROC of 87.20%	The study adequately predict T2DM
4	Kumari et al. (2021) [19]	Pima and breast cancer dataset	Min- max normalization, label encoding	Soft voting of LR, RF and NB	Soft voting classifier—accuracy 79.08% ,	A soft voting classifier model has been developed by combining three ML algorithms.
5	Huaping Zhou et al. (2020) [20]	Pima	Data cleaning and data transformation	Deep Learning Diabetes Prediction	Accuracy for diabetes type 94.02 % and for pima 99.41%	Designed DL diabetic prediction model predict diabetic future as well as type of diabetes i.e. T1/ T2 DM

6	Amine Rghioui, et al. (2020) [16]	sensor data and glucometer	not mentioned	NB, J48, SMO, RF ZeroR, OneR,	SMO gives superior classification accuracy compared to others	Developed a smart architecture for diabetic prediction using 5G technology.
7	N. P. Tigga et al. (2019) [8]	Pima, participants (age<18)	Data cleaning and data transformation	LR, KNN, SVM, NB, DT and RF	RF - 94.10%	The study identified significant diabetes variables and compared various ML algorithms.
8	Huma Naz (2019) [21]	Pima	LASSO	DL, ANN, NB, and DL, MDNN	Multilayer deep neural network 98.07%	Powered DL based system help doctors predict health outcomes more effectively
9	Talha Mahboob Alam et al. (2019) [7]	Pima	PCA	ANN, RF, k-means	ANN 75.7% accuracy	Prediction by selecting significant attributes and a strong relationship among BMI and BG level.
10	Souad Larabi-Marie- Sainte (2019) [22]	Pima	NB and LR based on Gaussian distribution	REPTree, M5P, SMO KSatar, OneR, ZeroR, BayesNet	74.48% highest accuracy attained by REPTree	Author reviewed current ML and DL diabetic prediction technique
11	Ravinder Ahuja et al. (2019) [23]	Pima	linear discriminant analysis (LDA)	RF, LR,SVC, DT, MLP	MLP accuracy 78.7%, recall 61.26%, precision 72.45% and F1 Score 65.97%	Presented a systematic approach to find the best-performing ML algorithm to predict diabetes.
12	Aishwarya Mujumdara et al. (2019) [24]	Pima Own dataset	Normalized BGL, Skin Thickness, BMI and Age values.	DT, GuasicianNB,LDA, SVC,RF, LR, ET, AB, BaGging, KNN	classification using LoR 96% and pipeline approach AB given 98% accuracy	Along with regular factors, the author has considered external factors, such as job style, for better diabetes classification.
13	Sneha N., Gangil, T. (2019) [25]	UCI machine repositoryory	attribute selection using correlation	DT, NB, SVM, RF, KNN	NB accuracy: 82.30%.	proposed good work performed the analysis of features in the dataset was conducted, and the optimal

						features were selected based on their correlation values.
14	Han Wu et al.(2018) [10]	Pima , Private Dataset	Normalized data using WEKA	K-means, LR	notable 3.04% accuracy gain was achieved by this model compared to existing prediction systems.	The proposed model enhances accuracy by using double level algorithms and next level classification is performed by using LoR.
15	Deepti Sisodiaa et al. (2018) [26]	Pima, online and offline questio nnaires	not mentioned	SVM, DT, NB	NB- 76.30%	Diabetes classification is performed using ML techniques based on the questionnaire designed
16	Ganjar Alfian et al. (2018) [27]	pima, own dataset	Apache kafka, MongoDB, NoSQL were used	RF, MLP, NB,SVM, LR Prediction-LSTM	Designed a model for Diabetes Prediction and Blood Glucose Monitoring	Early prediction of diabetes is performed using data generated from the BLE-based sensors
17	N. Yuvaraj et al. (2017) [28]	Pima	Information gain	DT, NB and RF	RF 94% accuracy	Hadoop- based clusters holds significant promise for diabetes prediction
18	Weifeng Xu et al. (2017) [29]	Private Dataset	dimensionalit y reduction, discretization	ID3, NB, RF, AB	RF Sensitivity is 100%	Investigate the relationship between readily available indicators and the risk of developing T2DM in young adults
19	Ali Mohebb, Tinna (2017) [9]	Private Dataset	normalization	LR, MLP, CNN	CCN with accuracy 77.5%	Study showed that, in addition to DL it is possible to detect T2D patients using CGM signals.
20	Nasib Singh Gill et al. (2016) [30]	Pima	max deviation feature selection method of	combining model of SVM and NN	96.06% accuracy using Hybrid Prediction Model (FS+SVM+NN)	The hybrid model attained a better accuracy rate than the individual techniques when applied in the same environment.

21	Neha Shukla &Meena Arora (2016) [31]	Pima	Not mentioned	NN,RF	RF precision: 92.96%	Scaled conjugate gradient have the slightest characterization exactness and RF tree give the better grouping precision results
22	J. P. Kandasamy et al. (2015) [32]	Pima	k-mean clustering	J48, KNN, SVF, RF	KNN and RF given 100% accuracy	Obtained results using PIMA with noisy and without noisy data
23	Aiswarya Iyer et al. 2015) [33]	Pima	Cfs Subset Eval algorithm	J48, NB	NB gives least error rates compared to J48	The study concluded that more methods should be compared to designing precise models.
24	Ebenezer Obalolu et al. (2014) [34]	Pima	Normalizatio n	BSS, EM algorithm, KNN, C4.5, BPNN	BPNN accuracy: 82%	The authors demonstrated the Effectiveness of Backpropagation in training an ANN for more accurate diabetes mellitus diagnosis.

2.2 Review of Blood Glucose Level Prediction

Recent trends in diabetes like use of CGM, closed loop technology using AI opened a new research area for prediction of BG levels to scientific researchers. BG level can be predicted for different horizons. Sophia Noel et. al. [35] reviewed various time series models like ARIMA, LSTM and Bi-LSTM. Her experimentation on the UVA/ Padova dataset proves that the Bi-LSTM model performed better.

Gómez-Castillo. et al. [36] proposed training a model to predict future BGLs with high precision using the OhioT1DM database and an LSTM network. Then the dataset is split into three different horizons. Study presents that time series results better than linear interpolation.

Bhimireddy et al. [37] developed individual models to predict BGLs in type 1 diabetes patients, including LSTM, BiLSTM, Convolutional LSTMs, TCN, and sequence-to-sequence models using CGM data. The experiments showed that a sequence-to-sequence BiLSTM outperformed the other models.

Recent trends in diabetes like use of CGM, closed loop technology using artificial intelligence opened a new research area for prediction of BG levels to scientific researchers. BG level can be predicted for different horizons. Wonju Seo et al. [38] developed a personalized BG level predictive model, based on a CNN. They utilized CGM datasets from 1052 professional CGM sessions and splitted T1DM, T2DM and GDM and predicted future BG levels of four different prediction horizons. Kim et al. [39] built a personalized glucose prediction model for hospitalized T2DM patients using DL. They compared three RNN architectures (simple RNN, GRU, and LSTM) using Dexcom G5 CGM data and found a simple GRU model with one RNN layer and two dense layers performed well.

McShinsky et al. [40] evaluated multiple ML methods for predicting glucose levels and glycemic events across 30- and 60-minute windows using 12 subjects from OhioT1DM. LASSO regression outperformed other techniques, yielding mean errors of 20.58 mg/dL (1.14 mmol/L) and 33.41 mg/dL (1.86 mmol/L) for the respective time frames.

Zhang et al. [41] benchmarked four data-driven approaches on OhioT1DM for 30- and 60-minute forecasts. Sequence-to-sequence LSTM achieved the lowest error (15.46 mg/dL or 0.86 mmol/L) for 30-minute predictions, though multiple linear regression proved more efficient for 60-minute forecasts (21.59 mg/dL or 1.2 mmol/L) while offering greater interpretability.

Zhu et al. [42] applied dilated recurrent networks with transfer learning to OhioT1DM, pre-training on combined datasets before specialization. This approach produced 18.9 mg/dL average error for 30-minute forecasts, outperforming standard recurrent architectures.

Rodriguez et al. [43] tested seven LSTM configurations with varying insulin and carbohydrate absorption models on D1NAMO. Their best-performing system reached 9.2 mg/dL (0.510 mmol/L) error for 60-minute predictions.

Arbi et al. [44] pursued non-invasive glucose estimation through cardiac signals. Using recurrent convolutional networks to process 1,600 D1NAMO ECG samples, they derived equations combining QT intervals, T-wave characteristics, and heart rate that achieved 0.0539 and 0.0602 mmol/L mean absolute errors.

Portable monitoring devices, internet of things, sensors, and wireless technology offer several advantages for diabetic patients including improved quality of life, reduced hospitalization time and reduced cost. Jayroop Ramesh et al. [45] designed a cloud-based system to merge patient information from personal health devices and wearables, demonstrating that an SVM-RBF model achieved a good accuracy of 83.20%.

Similarly, a personalized healthcare monitoring system was developed by Ganjar Alfian et al. [27] for leveraging individual data and information generated by Bluetooth Low Energy (BLE) sensor devices. For real-time processing of sensor data, Apache Kafka and MongoDB were utilized. An MLP-based algorithm classified diabetes patients, while LSTM predicted BGLs. Similarly,

Advances in glucose monitoring technology continue toward less invasive, more accessible solutions. Ilesanmi Daniyan et al. [46] created an affordable earlobe sensor using 1550nm near-infrared light, with Bluetooth connectivity to mobile devices, and demonstrated proportional glucose-to-signal correlation. Maria Valero et al. [47] validated a NIR spectroscopy prototype against human blood samples, reporting strong clinical accuracy. Paful Pai [48] built a portable photoacoustic spectroscopy system with FPGA processing and cloud integration for remote patient tracking.

The detailed review on recent studies performed by researchers in the field of prediction of BGL is presented in table 2.2. It highlights the dataset used, preprocessing techniques applied, and methods or algorithms used, along with results and findings.

Table 2.2. Summary of review in Prediction of BGL

Sr. No.	Author	Dataset/s & samples Used	Preprocessing & Feature Selection Technique	Methods/ algorithms	Results	Findings
1	Bian et al. (2024) [49]	8 diabetic patients,	normalization and calibration; lag sequence preparation	LSTM and attention-based model	MSE: 1.18 (15 min), 1.70 (30 min), 2.00 (45 min)	The hybrid model outperformed the standalone LSTM, effectively capturing long-term dependencies and short-term fluctuations for real-time CGM glucose forecasting.
2	Rajeswari et al. [50] (2024)	101 (diabetics)	Pre-processing included noise filtering, EDA, removal of artifacts from skin tone, ambient light, and pressure variations	Ridge Regression (RR), ML models	Accuracy: 99.02% ; MAE: 0.15 / 0.06; MSE: 0.22 / 0.006; 100%	Developed a low-cost, portable NIR-based prototype capable of continuous non-invasive glucose estimation with very high accuracy; robust to light and pressure effects.
3	Mehrad J. et al (2023) [51]	DIAdvisor datasets (59)	linear interpolation (cgm Gaps), normalization	Stacks of CNN and LSTM units (CNN-LSTM)	RMSE: 23.45±3.18 mg/dL (90 min PH)	The model successfully demonstrated performance for long-term prediction up to a 90-minute Prediction Horizon (PH).
4	Tabassum Khan, et	UCI	Weibull distribution	LiR, SVR model and	SVR- 3.24 mmol/ L	how data scarcity and high data variation affect BGL

	al. (2022) [52]		(WD) data fitting technique	WD model.	(RMSE)	
5	Han et al. (2022) [53]	1,410, T2D	Missing-value handling, clinical variable selection (LoR)	LoR	AUC = 0.715	Model effectively predicts perioperative hypoglycemia risk for surgical T2D patients
6	Wright et al. (2022) [54]	153, T1D	Data cleaning, feature extraction from insulin orders, temporal segmentation	XGBoost	AUC = 0.99	Insulin-order–centric models accurately predict inpatient hypoglycemia risk
7	Duckworth et al. (2022) [55]	153, T1D	Signal preprocessing, noise filtering; SHAP-based feature importance	Explainable ML Models (Tree-based)	AUC = 0.998,	Explainable ML supports personalized glucose control and transparent decision-making
8	Jayroop Ramesh Raafat A burukba (2021) [45]	Pima, Data collected from iHealth vendors-3	chi squared test, extremel y randomi sed trees classifier and LASSO , SMOTE	kNN, LR, Gaussian NB, and SVM - RBF	SVM-RBF accuracy 83.20 %, sensitivity 87.20%, and specificity 79%	Though the dataset is small but author provided an expanded view of real-time automated diabetes management systems by considering physiological factors.
9	Rabby et al. (2021) [56]	Ohio T1DM dataset	Kalman smoothing technique	Stacked LSTM	Average RMSE: 6.45 mg/dl (30 min PH)	The use of Kalman smoothing effectively improves reliability by mitigating CGM sensor errors, resulting in highly accurate 30 min prediction.
10	Calhoun et al. (2021) [57]	127 T1D	Normalization, repeated-measure adjustments	Repeated Measures Random Forest (RMRF)	AUC ≈ 0.78 (30 min)	RMRF effectively captured within-subject temporal variation

11	Wang et al. (2021) [58]	12 participants,	Smoothing, outlier removal, physiological parameter extraction	Ruan model, Hovorka model	Short-term prediction accuracy > 85% for 30–60 min horizon	Mixture model improved stability and nighttime prediction reliability
12	Kyi et al. (2021) [59]	94 participants with T2D	Missing-value handling, clinical feature selection	LoR	AUC = 0.806	Tool successfully stratified high-risk hospitalized T2D patients
13	Dae-Yeon Kim (2020) [39]	Data from Soonchunhyang University	removed records for missing values and outliers	RNN, GRU, LSTM	A GRU-based model with one recurrent and two dense layers effectively predicted BGL	A model was developed to analyze individual patients' BGL to identify patterns, and generate personalized predictions of future values.
14	Jagruti Prajapati et al. (2020) [60]	Ohio T1DM (12), Padova	Missing imputation, Normalization, forward fill for insulin	BiLSTM	16.45 mg/dl for the 60-minute prediction horizon (pH-60 min)	Bi-LSTM networks are effective for blood glucose prediction using CGM measurements, with the bidirectional structure enhancing context understanding.
15	Vehí et al. [2020] [61]	10 (41 years), 6 (40–60 years) T1D participants	CGM smoothing, noise filtering, feature extraction	GE, SVM, AN	Sensitivity > 80%; prediction horizon up to 30 min	ML gave early-warning capability with clinically significant lead time
16	Stuart et al. (2017) [62]	9,584 diabetics	Handling missing EHR values, clinical variable selection	Bootstrapping	AUC = 0.73	Helps clinicians identify high-risk hospitalized patients, improving inpatient safety
17	Plis, K., (2014) [63]	5 T1D, 200	feature engineering from physiological model outputs	SVR	ARIMA RMSE: 19.8 mg/dL (30 min), 38.4 mg/dL (60 min)	SVR with physiologic features achieved superior predictive accuracy over ARIMA and clinical experts, detecting ~25% of hypoglycemic events 30 min ahead.

2.3 Review of Prediction of Diabetes Complications

Predictive modeling helps identify diabetes risks and forecast complications beyond simple diagnosis. Zhou and Myrzashova [20] developed a system that predicts the likelihood of diabetes and identifies which disease subtype may develop. Georga et al. [64] built a monitoring platform where patients log daily measurements and receive tailored warnings about impending hypo- or hyperglycemic episodes.

T. Khan et al. [52] proposed three prediction models—LiR, support vector regression (SVR), and WD —each using the current and previous days' blood glucose to forecast the next day's fasting BG level.The 70 patients CGM dataset was used from several weeks to months. Among three developed models, the SVR model results better with an average 3.24 mmol/L RMSE

Using 884 patient records containing 79 clinical variables, Yazan Jian et al. [65] trained models to forecast eight common complications: metabolic syndrome, dyslipidemia, neuropathy, nephropathy, diabetic foot, hypertension, obesity, and retinopathy. Their approach correctly classified cases 97.8% of the time.

Mathieu Ravaut et al. [66] developed a ML model to predict the three-year risk of adverse outcomes due to diabetes complications. This model can help health planners and decision-makers allocate healthcare resources more effectively for diabetes management.

M. V. Kabyshev et. al. [67] developed a client-server system for with Diabetic mellitus. They designed the app which works with Apple's platforms HealthKit, Research Kit and CareKit with iOS operating systems ecosystem. By doing cluster analysis they have identified groups of patients based on similarities and possible diabetes complications. Diabetes prediction was carried out by applying RF.

2.4 Summary of Findings

The following section will discuss conclusions marked from literature review in the field of prediction of diabetes and predictions of BGLs using.

2.4.1 Machine Learning and Ensemble Based Approaches

There has been considerable effort in applying addressing ML to structured data sets such as the Pima Indians Diabetes Dataset (PIDD), test results from laboratories, as well as electronic health data records. Some examples of these learning algorithms would be LoR, SVM, NB, KNN, DT, and RF.

One of the first models used in predicting the binary classifications of diabetes is LoR due to its simplicity and interpretability. In some instances though, its predictive power is often hindered in the case of complicated continuous patterns. More sophisticated nonlinear patterns are managed with SVMs because of its use of kernel functions to map the input features into optimal higher dimensional spaces, to try and achieve better separation of the diabetic classes. NB is fast and does well for smaller estates, however, the independence assumption comes into play to limit flexibility. There is also the option of DT, which is predictive and rule based (very intuitive), however, overfitting does happen.

There is consistent evidence from the literature to affirm that RF, which is an ensemble of DT, has the best performance due to the reduction of the variance with the ability to manage the noise in the features effectively. KNN also shows simplicity, however, it is heavily based on the choice of "k" and the distance metric. In general, ML models exhibit decent performance on well-preprocessed datasets, achieving accuracies between 70% and 85%, though their capability to model highly complex relationships remains limited.

Ensemble learning methods are being used more and more for diabetes prediction since they improve predictive power by merging different weak and/or strong learners. Popular ensemble learning methods include: Bagging, Boosting, Stacking, and more advanced methods such as RF, AB, Gradient Boosting Machines (GBM), XGBoost, LightGBM, and CatBoost.

Bagging methods, primarily RF, lower variance in the prediction by fitting multiple DT to different bootstrapped samples. RF is a popular method in medical classification tasks as it is robust and stable. AB and GB, which are methods of Boosting, construct and improve classifiers sequentially by focusing on previously misclassified examples in the training set. Recent methods such as XGBoost, LightGBM, and CatBoost show improved performance in comparison to classical ML methods as they are more accurate, have lower bias, and are better at missing data.

More advanced methods of stacking involve one or more levels of models, where the predictions of primary models (SVM, KNN, RF) are combined by a meta-learner (LoR) to form a single predictive unit. Stacked ensembles usually provide better generalization and performance on complex, multi-class classification tasks. Such ensembles perform diabetes classification with accuracy in the 85-95% range which surpasses standard classifiers.

2.4.2 Deep Learning Approach for Blood Glucose Prediction Models

DL has become one of the most common techniques to predicting diabetes using large, complex and multimodal datasets like clinical narratives, CGM signals and other physiological data. Out of the different architectures of DL, the most common ones are ANN, CNN, RNNs, LSTM networks, GRUs and convolutional-recurrent hybrid models.

Feedforward based ANNs are the basis of most architectures in prediction tasks of DL. While they are quite promising, they should be approached with caution because they are prone to overfitting, especially when the prediction task has a limited dataset. Review shows that CNNs are not just perfect for images but the extracts required features from health records too. In the predicting of the glucose levels over time, several LSTM and GRUs are required to accurately analyze the data because of the time dependencies and the complex Glucose levels. LSTM Networks have been specifically developed to manage the vanishing gradient problem by storing long term memory in sequences [68]. GRU Models made LSTM architectures simpler while obtaining similar outcomes with less computational complexity [69]. CNN-LSTM hybrid models incorporate convolutional layers for spatial feature extraction and LSTM layers for temporal modeling to facilitate multivariate sensor inputs.

When used on rich time-series data derived from wearable sensors or CGM, these models will probably be more beneficial, as the models explicitly learn long-range temporal dynamics, something that likely enhances predictive performance.

Correctly predicting glucose is important for good diabetes management, as it can provide input into decision-making regarding insulin doses, the timing of meals, and physical activity. The traditional approach for considering these factors in decisions regarding glucose regulation has been carbohydrate counting (or heuristics). Glucose dynamics is influenced by several factors (e.g., carbohydrate intake, rolling of insulin, exercise, circadian rhythm, stress, and illness) and is both non-linear and time-varying. Given this context, traditional regression models do not frequently lend themselves to the generation of accurate and reliable predictions.

Key challenges remain in achieving high accuracy over longer prediction horizons and handling the high inter- and intra-patient variability influenced by factors like stress, illness, and unannounced meals.

Overall, the progression from traditional ML to ensemble learning and then to advanced DL models reflects the field's evolution toward more accurate and robust diabetes prediction systems. As a rule, DL approaches generally also have greater sensitivity and specificity than classical machine-learning disease models with clinical relevance but are highly reliant on high-quality and large datasets. While ML models remain valuable for their interpretability and ease of implementation, ensemble and DL approaches achieve superior predictive accuracy, making them promising candidates for integration into clinical decision-support systems. DL methods also require significant investment in both computational resources and hyperparameter tuning. The lack of transparency associated with DL models has fueled interest in the development of more interpretable algorithms that can be more easily understood and "trusted" by clinicians. The continued growth of wearable technologies and large-scale health records is expected to further accelerate the development of high-performance predictive models.

2.5 Research Gap

Despite significant advancements in ML techniques for diabetes prediction and blood glucose forecasting, current models primarily focus on:

1. There is evidence that effective interventions can improve diabetes management and reduce modifiable risk factors, but significant gaps remain in the knowledge base.
2. Researchers with medical professionals together identify the most important and dependent parameters for diabetic prediction. So, more accurate results will be generated.
3. Many researchers have developed models for diabetic prediction, but more focus is required to promote patient health activities and their diet.
4. To predict the patient's BGL more focus should be required by considering the patients' behavioral, lifestyle, activity, and health-related aspects.

5. Some studies missed the mark. They didn't really focus on things like how people choose their meals, the role of tech in diabetes education, or even simple medication reminders. But these are key pieces for anyone dealing with diabetes.
6. There is less amount of work to be carried out on real-time data generated by sensors or wearable devices.It is necessary that the performance of decision-making systems be sufficiently high and resistant to loads from a big number of different clients.
7. While finding the accurate ML methods, the execution time for building and validation with feature selection needs to be considered.
8. Large systems should constantly have documentation. There is a real need to manage the process and product of development.
9. A lot of ML models never make it out of the lab. They just sit in research papers, without solid testing in real hospitals, so doctors can't actually use them.
10. It's a real headache trying to get everything working smoothly together. Hybrid algorithms are being developed and researched to have a more accurate and reliable forecast of BGLs, especially in people suffering from diabetes.

Therefore, to respond to the demands of future intelligent e-health technologies, this research successfully developed and validated a dual-pronged strategy for diabetes management, which includes a highly accurate diabetes prediction model and a robust BGL forecasting system.

2.6 Research Objectives

Diabetes management is a complex, highly individualized process consisting of ongoing monitoring and immediate decision-making about diet, exercise, and medication. Old methods based on past information and sporadic clinical visits are not well suited to deliver anticipatory and preemptive care. But with the development of multi-sensor devices like CGMs and wearables, patient-specific information has proliferated. This offers a historical opportunity to use ML and DL to transition from reactive care to a new era of predictive, personalized diabetes management.

This study aims to develop a Diabetes prediction framework alongside a BGL forecasting framework that employs advanced computational methods to enhance glucose predictions, enable early detection, and support preventive healthcare measures. The overarching goal is to design and evaluate a Hybrid DL Framework that blends traditional ML with advanced DL techniques for comprehensive diabetes and glucose prediction.

To achieve this, the project has the following master goals:

1. To study and compare ML algorithms for diabetes predictions.
2. To develop, evaluate, and compare the performance of ensemble models for diabetes prediction.
3. To build a deep learning model capable of predicting blood glucose levels using historical data.
4. Facilitate patient-specific glucose data analysis and visualization.
5. To predict the likelihood of diabetes-related complications.
6. To determine risk factors of diabetes.

CHAPTER 3
DATASETS

This chapter provides a brief overview of the four diabetes-related datasets, of which three are used to predict diabetes, and one is used to predict BGL, as will be discussed later in the chapter.

3.1 Datasets Used for Diabetes Prediction

This section outlines the publicly available diabetes datasets listed in Table 3.1, which served as the foundation for the experimental analysis. Three datasets were selected for evaluation: the Pima Indian Diabetes dataset, the Neha Tigga dataset, and a general diabetes dataset. The Pima Indian dataset, a well-established benchmark in medical research, includes diagnostic data from female patients of Pima Indian descent and is frequently used in classification studies. The Neha Tigga dataset, compiled for academic purposes, contains structured patient records with clinically relevant features, enabling comparative analysis across different ML techniques. The general diabetes dataset offers a wider range of patient information, contributing to diversity in both demographic and clinical variables. Collectively, these datasets provided a comprehensive framework for assessing model performance across varied data characteristics and distributions.

Table 3.1. Publicly Available Diabetes Datasets

Sr. No	Dataset Name	No. of attributes	No. of samples	URL
1	Pima Diabetes Dataset [70]	9	768	https://archive.ics.uci.edu/ml/
2	Diabetes Dataset [71]	16	100	https://data.mendeley.com/datasets/wj9rwkp9c2/1
3	Neha Tigga Dataset [72]	18	952	https://www.kaggle.com/datasets/tigganeha4/diabetes-dataset-2019

3.1.1. Pima Indian Diabetes Dataset: Dataset 1

The predictive analysis in this study utilizes data provided by the National Institute of Diabetes and Digestive and Kidney Diseases (NIDDK). This dataset was designed to support diagnostic assessments of diabetes in patients using a range of clinical measurements. It includes records of female individuals aged 21 and above, with eight input features: number of pregnancies, body mass index (BMI), insulin levels, age, plasma glucose concentration, skinfold thickness, diastolic blood pressure, and diabetes pedigree function as shown in table 3.2. The target variable is binary, indicating diabetic status as either 1 (positive) or 0 (negative). Widely adopted in medical data research, the Pima dataset has served as a benchmark for evaluating classification models. It comprises 768 patient records, all of which represent adult women. Among these, 268 individuals (34.90%) are diagnosed with diabetes, while 500 (65.10%) are non-diabetic, as determined by the diagnostic attributes included in the dataset.

Table 3.2 Feature description of Pima dataset

Sr. No.	Features	Description	Measuring Unit	Type of Data	Value Range
1	pregnancy	No. of times pregnancy	-	Discrete	[0-17]
2	Body Mass Index	The BMI is weight in kilograms divided by height in meters squared	kg/m^2	Continuous	[0-67]
3	Insulin Level	2h serum insulin	U/ml	Continuous	[0-846]
4	Age	Age of an individual	years	Discrete	[21-81]
5	Glucose Concentration	This test checks your blood sugar levels. It should be tested before fasting and after fasting	mg/dl	Continuous	[0-199]
6	Diastolic	measures the pressure in your arteries when your heart rests between beats	mm	Continuous	[0-122]
7	Triceps skin fold thickness	determined by collagen content and is increased in insulin-dependent diabetes mellitus	mu	Continuous	[0-99]
8	Diabetes pedigree function	A function that scores lthe ikelihood of diabetes based on family history	-	Continuous	[0-2.45]
9	class	Diabetic/non-diabetic	-	Discrete	0/1

3.1.2. Neha Tigga Dataset: Dataset 2

The author has collected 952 instances through an online and offline questionnaire, which includes 218 questions as mentioned in table 3.3. The experimentation was conducted for the prediction of T2D.

Table 3.3. Feature description of Neha Tigga Dataset

Sr. No.	Parameters	Instances	Sr. No.	Parameters	Instances
1	Age	18 or above	12	Hours of sleep	Numeric
2	Alcohol consumption	Yes/ No	13	Regular intake of medicine?	Yes/ No
3	Male	580	14	Junk food	Yes/ No
4	Female	372	15	Frequency of urination	Not much Quite much
5	Family history with diabetes	Yes/ No			
6	Diagnosed with high BP	Yes/ No	16	BP Level	High/ normal/ low
7	Walk/ run/ physically	None	17	Number of pregnancies	Numeric
		Less than half an hour	18	Gestational diabetes	Yes/ No
		More than half an hour	19	Stress	Not at all
		One hour or more			Sometimes
8	BMI	Numeric	20		Often
9	Smoking	Yes/ No			Always
10	Gender	Male/ Female	21	Diabetic	Diabetic - 267 Non diabetic - 685
11	Hours of sound sleep	Numeric			

3.1.3 Diabetes Dataset: Dataset 3

This data was acquired from the laboratory of Medical City Hospital, Iraqi society. The data consists of a total 1000 patients medical information and laboratory analysis. The dataset that has been created from this data contains the parameters mentioned in table 3.4. The database includes 103 non diabetic and 53 pre-diabetic and 844 diabetic patients.

Table 3.4. Feature description of Diabetes Dataset

Sr. No.	Attributes	Description	Mean ± Std.
1	Gender	0 for females and 1 for male	0.565 ± 0.4958
2	Age	Age (20-79) in years	53.739 ± 8.8557
3	Fasting blood sugar (FBS)	result of a blood sample taken after a patient fasted for at least eight hours (mmol/l)	10.1443 ± 5.0844
4	High blood urea nitrogen (BUN)	BUN is the amount of urea nitrogen that's in your blood (mmol/l)	5.1808 ± 3.3486
5	Chromium (Cr)	blood levels of chromium (mmol/l)	69.28 ± 62.2764
6	Chol	Fast Cholesterol levels (mmol/l)	4.9092 ± 2.004
7	TG	Concentration of Triglyceride Levels (mmol/l)	2.3506 ± 1.3988
8	LDL	Low-Density Lipoprotein (mmol/l)	2.6145 ± 1.1175
9	HDL	High-Density Lipoprotein (mmol/l)	1.2067 ± 0.6594
10	BMI	Body Mass Index (Weight in kg / (Height in m)^2)	29.4255 ± 4.8553

11	Gyrated hemoglobin (HBA1C)	For the previous two to three months, average blood glucose (sugar) levels (mmol/l)	8.2623 ± 2.5370
12	Class	Diabetic/non diabetic/ pre diabetic	

3.2 Tools and Techniques used for data collection

This section discusses the technology and devices used for capturing the D1NAMO dataset.

3.2.1 Diabetes Technology

Diabetes technology is used to help and better manage diabetics' BGLs, stave off diabetes complications, reduce the burden of living with diabetes, and also improve the quality of life [20]. During the past 30 years, diabetes management has witnessed significant changes in glucose measurement, insulin administration, and types of insulin. These changes have improved the lives of people with diabetes [11]. Technological transformation helps diabetes patients to manage their health with digital devices to track, monitor, and even share lifestyle data generated with healthcare professionals. Several technologies, such as continuous glucose monitoring, self-monitoring blood glucose devices, CGM with automatically controlled insulin delivery, glucose monitoring technologies, and mobile devices have facilitated ongoing improvements in self-care and communication of data [15]. Wang Y. et al. [73], discussed different diabetic technologies and tools organized from low to high-tech solutions, which can improve care for diabetic patients [17]. Technology also has led to improvements in outcomes such as HbA1c, hypoglycemia events, and quality of life while importantly empowering people to self-manage their diabetes. Recently, diabetes technology has expanded to hybrid devices that monitor glucose levels, deliver insulin, as well as software that serves as a medical device for providing diabetes self-management support. Several trends are emerging in glucose monitoring as follows:

3.2.2. Continuous Glucose Monitor (CGM)

CGM measures BGLs continuously and updates the glucose level display every 5 minutes intervals. CGMs consist of a display monitor, a sensor that is inserted into the subcutaneous tissue, and a transmitter that transmits the sensor data to the monitor. These devices help to get real-time BGLs and get continuous feedback on diet, exercise, and insulin requirements. But sensors need to be replaced after every 10 to 90 days, depending on the CGM system providers. By combining data from multiple patients, trends can be found between people and general patterns can be identified. Ganjar Alfian et al. [27] uncovered that the FDA had accepted CGM sensors for monitoring glucose in different trends and patterns. The study carried out by Ali Mohebbi et al. [11] showed the possible use of CGM signals for adherence detection for T2D patients, in addition to DL being a promising approach for this task. The most probably used CGM devices are Abbott, Dexcom, Libre, and Medtronic Guardian.

3.3 Dataset Used for BGL Prediction: D1NAMO Dataset

D1NAMO is a publicly available dataset [74] designed to support research on non-invasive management for T1DM. The dataset provides real-world CGM data for Type 1 Diabetes patients. It contains multivariate physiological and behavioral parameters collected from wearable sensors, insulin pumps, and manual records. The D1NAMO dataset was acquired over 4 days. This extended data collection period was crucial for capturing the variability in BGL and other physiological parameters that can occur over time, especially in individuals with T1DM [25]. The dataset includes data from 20 healthy subjects and 9 (6 men and 3 women) with T1DM, in real-life conditions, using the Zephyr BioHarness 3 wearable chest-belt device as shown in figure 3.1. The age range for 9 diabetics range from 20 to 39 years. The acquisition of physiological signals—ECG, breathing, and accelerometer outputs—has been made using the Zephyr Bioharness 3 device. The key features of the dataset include electrocardiogram recordings, respiratory rate and patterns, movement data, CGM readings (at every 5 minutes of interval), and pictures of consumed meals with annotations. The total 8414 CGM recordings acquired for 9 diabetics across the four days. The food details of each patient is also recorded (average 3 times in day), as shown in figure 3.2 for patient ID 2. Annotations of food images by a dietitian are valuable in the context of calorie estimation, as they impact glucose levels. All data points are synchronized with precise timestamps, enabling accurate correlation and analysis.

Figure 3.1: Zephyr BioHarness 3.0 ECG, electrocardiography
(Image Source:
https://www.researchgate.net/publication/350545515_HRV_in_Active-Duty_Special_Forces_and_Public_Order_Military_Personnel)

Figure 3.2: Food Image 014 of subject 1
(Image Source: https://doi.org/10.1016/j.imu.2018.09.003)

CHAPTER 4
TECHNIQUES FOR DIABETES PREDICTION AND BLOOD GLUCOSE LEVEL PREDICTION

This section briefs the ML and ensemble methods used for diabetes prediction in the first half, and in the second half, it introduces DL methods used for BGL prediction.

4.1 Machine Learning Methods for Diabetes Prediction

To establish reliable benchmarks for diabetes prediction, a comparative study was conducted using several traditional ML algorithms. KNN, SVM, NB, DT, and LoR are frequently used for diabetes prediction primarily because they are efficient at binary classification, offer high interpretability, and work well with the structured datasets. These models were selected for their interpretability, diversity in learning strategies, and proven effectiveness in classification tasks. Each algorithm was trained on the diabetes datasets and evaluated using key performance metrics such as accuracy, precision, recall, and F1-score. The insights gained from this evaluation informed the design and calibration of the ensemble models.

4.1.1 Decision Tree (DT) [75]

Decision Trees are hierarchical models that split data based on feature values to arrive at a classification decision. They are intuitive and easy to interpret but prone to overfitting. For this experiment, a Gini index-based DT was trained to serve as both a standalone classifier and a base learner for ensemble methods. Its performance helped assess the trade-off between model simplicity and predictive power. The entropy and gini index is calculated as:

Entropy:

$$Entropy = \sum_{i=0}^{n} - \rho_i log_2 \rho_i \tag{4.1}$$

Gini Index:

$$Gin\, i_i = 1 - \sum_{k=1}^{n} (\rho_i, k)^2 \tag{4.2}$$

n represents the number of distinct class values.

4.1.2 Naive Bayes (NB) [76]

It is a probabilistic classifier that applies Bayes' theorem as shown equation 3.4 under the assumption of conditional independence among features. Despite its simplicity, it is computationally efficient and often performs well on high-dimensional data. For this experiment, the Gaussian variant of NB was applied to the datasets. It served as a lightweight baseline model, offering a contrast to more complex classifiers and contributing to ensemble diversity.

Bayes' Theorem:

$$P(C|X) = \frac{P(C).P(C)}{P(X)} \tag{4.3}$$

4.1.3 Logistic Regression (LoR) [77]

It is a linear model used for binary classification tasks. It estimates the probability of class membership by applying a sigmoid function (equation 3.5) to a linear combination of input features. In this work, LoR was trained to model the relationship between clinical attributes and diabetes outcomes. Its probabilistic output was particularly useful for soft voting and calibration stages, where refined probability estimates were essential.

Sigmoid Function:

$$P(Y = 1|X) = \frac{1}{1+e^{-(\beta_0+\beta_1 \beta X_1+....+\beta_n \beta X_n)}} \tag{4.4}$$

4.1.4 AdaBoost (AB) [78]

AdaBoost is a boosting algorithm that combines multiple weak learners, typically decision stumps, in a sequential manner. Each learner focuses on correcting the errors of its predecessor by adjusting the weights of misclassified instances. In this study, AdaBoost was implemented to evaluate its ability to improve classification performance through iterative refinement. Its inclusion provided insight into how boosting compares to bagging-based methods like RF in the context of medical data.

4.1.5 Random Forest (RF) [79]

It is an ensemble-based classifier that constructs multiple DT using bootstrapped samples and random feature selection at each split. This approach reduces overfitting and enhances generalization by ensuring diversity among the trees. In this study, the RF model was trained on the preprocessed datasets, and its performance was assessed based on its ability to handle feature interactions and imbalanced data. Its robustness and relatively high accuracy made it a strong candidate for inclusion in the ensemble phase.

4.1.6 K-Nearest Neighbor (KNN) [80]

KNN is a non-parametric algorithm that classifies instances based on the majority label among their k closest neighbors, using distance metrics such as Euclidean distance. In this study, KNN was applied to evaluate how well local instance-based learning performs on the diabetes datasets. The value of k was optimized through cross-validation, and the model's sensitivity to feature scaling was addressed during preprocessing.

Euclidean Distance:

$$d(x, y) = \sqrt{\sum_{i=1}^{n} (x_i - y_i)^2} \tag{4.5}$$

These models were trained and evaluated using key performance metrics such as accuracy, precision, recall, and F1-score. The comparative analysis provided a foundation for the subsequent ensemble learning stage.

4.1.7. Linear Discriminant Analysis (LDA) [81]

LDA is a supervised classification method widely used in statistical analysis. It selects a linear combination of input features that best separates several classes of a dataset. The procedure determines a set of discriminant functions that provides the best separation between the classes while minimizing the variation within the class. In principle, it calculates the direction of the feature space where data groups can be most distinctly separated. This technique implicitly assumes that data follows a normal distribution and that class covariance matrices are equal, and the separation between classes can be described by a linear frontier.

4.1.8 Gradient Boosting Classifier (GBC) [82]

It is a tree-based ML technique designed to improve the accuracy of the model. The general principle underlying it, boosting, combines several weak learners in order to create a strong predictive model. It starts with developing an initial DT on the features of the dataset for evaluating the performance of the model. It then calculates the error or misclassification between the predicted and actual values. After that, new trees are iteratively built to minimize those errors; each new DT centers on the residuals or mistakes of the previously built one. In successive steps, the model gets closer and closer to the actual until the error becomes negligible or stabilized.

4.1.9. CatBoost Classifier [83]

CatBoost is an advanced gradient boosting algorithm to handle categorical and numerical data efficiently. Among these, its main strength is that it can process categorical variables directly, without needing to apply one-hot or label encoding, as in traditional methods.

Unlike many other models that require extensive preprocessing, CatBoost automatically normalizes feature values internally, thereby simplifying the preparation of data. In addition, for improved generalization and avoidance of overfitting, it implements regularization methods, including L1 and L2 penalties. Taken together, these features make CatBoost a very powerful, user-friendly tool for the purposes of building high-performance predictive models.

4.2 Ensemble Methods for Diabetes Prediction

To improve the reliability and accuracy of diabetes prediction, this study explored two ensemble learning techniques [84]: stacking and voting classifiers. These methods combine the strengths of multiple individual models to produce more robust predictions.

4.2.1 Stacking

Stacking is a layered ensemble approach that integrates predictions from several base models through a secondary model known as the meta-learner as shown in Figure 4.1. The process begins with training multiple classifiers—either of the same type with different configurations or entirely different algorithms—on the original dataset. Each base model generates its own predictions, which are then used as input features for the meta-model. This second-level model learns how to best combine the outputs of the base models to produce the final prediction.

Unlike bagging or boosting, which rely on repeated sampling or sequential error correction, stacking operates through a two-stage learning process. It is particularly effective in capturing complementary patterns across diverse classifiers, thereby reducing individual model biases and improving overall performance.

4.2.2 Voting Classifiers

Voting classifiers aggregate predictions from multiple models to arrive at a final decision. This method is based on the principle that combining diverse perspectives can lead to more accurate outcomes. Two types of voting strategies were implemented in this study: soft voting and hard voting.

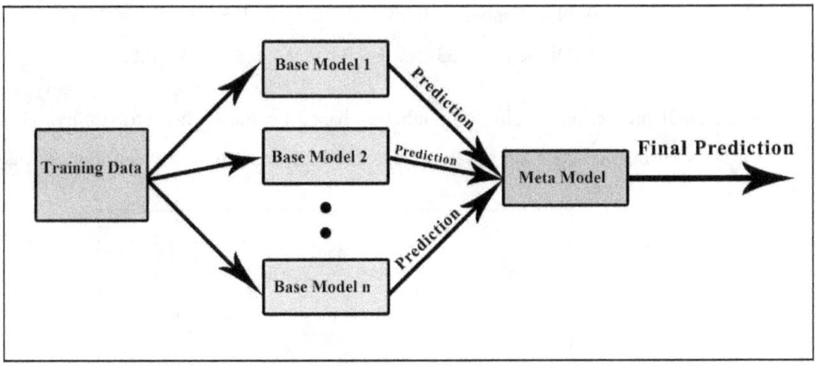

Figure 4.1. Stacking

4.2.2.1 Soft Voting

Soft voting combines the probability estimates from each classifier rather than their final class labels. These probabilities are averaged—either equally or with assigned weights—and the class with the highest combined probability is selected as shown in figure 4.2. This technique is especially useful when classifiers vary in confidence levels, as it accounts for the strength of each prediction.

For example, consider three classifiers (M1, M2, M3) predicting the likelihood of diabetes for a given patient:

- M1 → [0.2, 0.8]
- M2 → [0.1, 0.9]
- M3 → [0.8, 0.2]

Assuming equal weights of 0.33, the combined probabilities are:

Class 0 (Non-Diabetic): $0.33 \times 0.2 + 0.33 \times 0.1 + 0.33 \times 0.8 = 0.363$

Class 1 (Diabetic): $0.33 \times 0.8 + 0.33 \times 0.9 + 0.33 \times 0.2 = 0.627$

The final prediction would be "Diabetic" based on the higher probability. This method allows for nuanced decision-making, especially in cases with overlapping or noisy data.

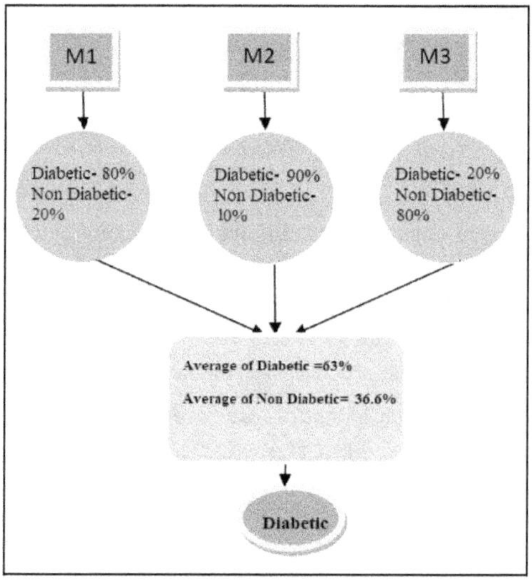

Figure 4.2: Soft Voting Classifier

4.2.2.2 Hard Voting

Hard voting, also known as majority voting, selects the class label that receives the most votes from individual classifiers [85]. Each model contributes one vote, and the class with the highest count becomes the final prediction as shown in Figure 4.3. This method is straightforward and effective for categorical outcomes.

For instance, if three classifiers produce the following predictions:

- M1 → Diabetic
- M2 → Non-Diabetic
- M3 → Diabetic

The ensemble output would be "Diabetic" since it appears most frequently. While hard voting does not consider prediction confidence, it offers simplicity and robustness in balanced datasets.

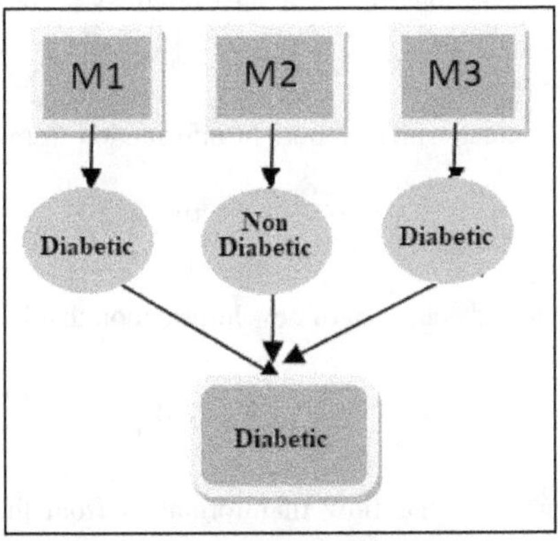

Figure 4.3: Hard Voting Classifier

4.3 Deep Learning and Hybrid Methods for Blood Glucose Prediction

The DL and hybrid methods mentioned below are used for the prediction of continuous BGLs.

4.3.1 Long Short-Term Memory (LSTM)

It is a powerful recurrent neural network architecture designed for processing and forecasting sequential data [68]. Its main strength lies in its ability to manage information flow over long sequences, allowing it to learn long-term dependencies. LSTM's ability to selectively remember, update, and use information over long sequences is its key strength, making it ideal for tasks involving sequential data. LSTM network uses a sophisticated architecture of gates and states to effectively manage information flow, solving the problem of vanishing gradients and enabling the network to learn long-term dependencies in sequential data. It mainly has three gates at any time instant, as shown in figure 4.4:

Forget gate: Decides which amount of information from the previous cell state to keep or discard.

$$F_t = \sigma(X_t W_{xf} + H_{t-1} W_{hf} + b_f) \quad (4.6)$$

Input gate: manages the amount of new information that is allowed to enter the cell state.

$$I_t = \sigma(X_t W_{xi} + H_{t-1} W_{hi} + b_i) \quad (4.7)$$

Output gate: governs the flow of information from the internal memory cell to the output.

$$O_t = \sigma(X_t W_{xo} + H_{t-1} W_{ho} + b_o) \quad (4.8)$$

It maintains both a cell state and a hidden state.

Cell State: A dedicated memory that runs through the entire sequence, storing information over long periods.

$$C_t = F_t \odot C_{t-1} + I_t \odot \tilde{C}_t \tag{4.9}$$

Hidden State: The output of the cell at the current time step, which is also passed to the next.

$$H_t = O_t \odot tanh(C_t) \tag{4.10}$$

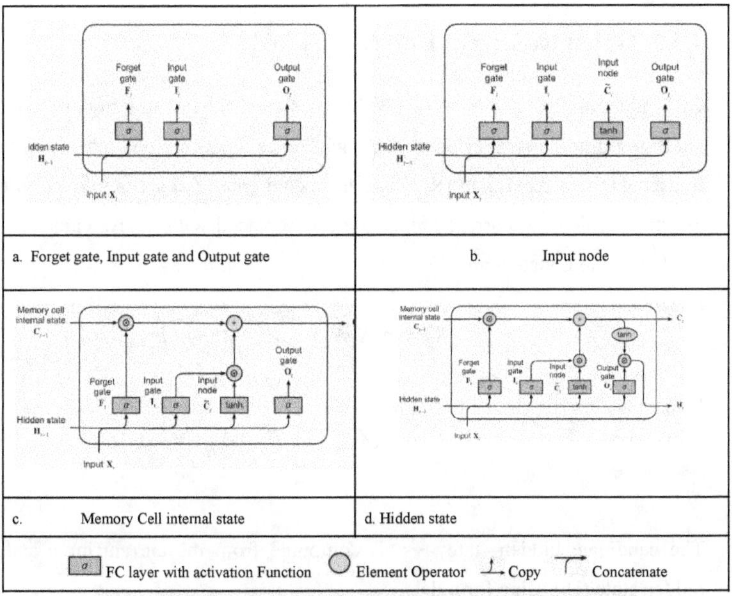

Figure 4.4: Computing different states of the LSTM model

These gates use sigmoid activation (σ) and weighted inputs ([ht-1, xt] concatenated) with biases. A candidate cell state (C̃t) is created using a tanh activation function as:

$$\tilde{C}_t = tanh(X_t W_{xc} + H_{t-1} W_{hc} + b_c) \tag{4.11}$$

The new cell state (C_t) is then updated by combining the forgotten information and the new input information. Finally, the hidden state (H_t) is evaluated using the output gate and the tanh of the current cell state. This process, illustrated in figure 5.4, allows LSTMs to manage information flow and learn long-term dependencies.

4.3.2 Gated Recurrent Unit (GRU) [69]

GRU is a simplified version of LSTMs, designed for fast training and good handling of vanishing gradients. The forget and input gates are combined into a single update gate. Subsequently, a reset gate (R_t) and an update gate (Z_t) are employed to determine the extent to which the current hidden state is replaced with a new value. The formula for reset gate and update gate is:

Reset Gate:

$$R_t = \sigma(X_t W_{xr} + H_{t-1} W_{hr} + b_r) \tag{4.12}$$

Update Gate:

$$Z_t = \sigma(X_t W_{xz} + H_{t-1} W_{hz} + b_z) \tag{4.13}$$

The candidate hidden state $\tilde{\mathbf{H}}_t$ is computed from the current input and the previous hidden state (H_t) using formulas

$$\tilde{H}_t = tanh(X_t W_{xh} + R_t \odot H_{t-1}) W_{hh} + b_c) \tag{4.14}$$

$$H_t = Z_t \odot H_{t-1} + (1 - Z_t) \odot \tilde{H}_t \quad (4.15)$$

This streamlined structure, as shown in figure 4.5, makes GRUs computationally more efficient than LSTMs.

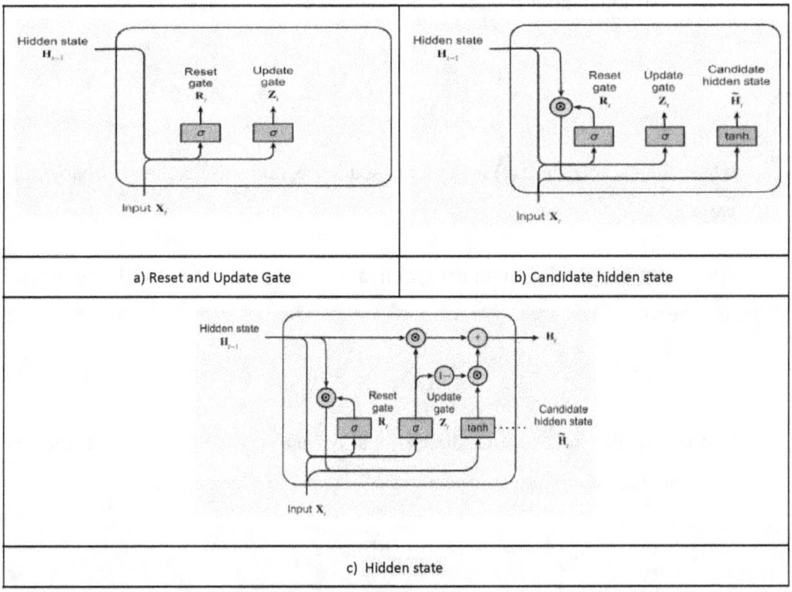

Figure 4.5: Computing different steps of the GRU Model

4.3.3 Convolutional Neural Network (CNN) [86]

CNN are a type of DL model that automatically finds important patterns in structured data like images or signals over time. CGM signals, along with other physiological measurements, often require structured feature extraction before they can be used for prediction tasks. Convolutional neural networks (CNNs) are well-suited for this purpose because they can automatically identify local patterns within sequential data.

The core operation in a CNN is the convolution, in which the kernel or filter is applied over the input to generate feature maps. Mathematically, the convolution operation for one-dimensional input signal (t) with kernel (k) can be given by:

$$y(t) = (x * w)(t) = \sum_{k=0}^{k=1} x(t + k).\, w(k) \tag{4.16}$$

where the kernel size, $x(t)$ is the input sequence, and $w(k)$ are the learnable filter weights.

After convolution, a nonlinear activation function like ReLU is applied to add nonlinearity

$$f(z) = max(0, z) \tag{4.17}$$

Pooling layers reduce the dimensionality and preserve the dominant features. For example, max pooling over a window of size p is defined as:

$$y_i = 1\epsilon[i,\, i + \rho]maxx_j \tag{4.18}$$

Features extracted are then fed into fully connected layers or combined with sequential models (e.g., LSTM, GRU) to learn long-range dependencies. This hybrid architecture uses CNNs for the extraction of local features and a recurrent structure to model temporal relationships, which will enhance the accuracy and robustness of glucose forecasting.

CHAPTER 5
EXPERIMENTAL SETUP

With the growing volume of electronic health records and patient-related data, computational techniques have emerged as essential tools for identifying patterns and aiding clinical decision-making. This research aims to assess the effectiveness of various ML and ensemble models in predicting diabetes, utilizing three distinct datasets to ensure the reliability and breadth of the findings. In addition to this, the prediction of BGL is also performed using the D1NAMO dataset.

Model A: Comparative Analysis of Different Diabetes Datasets Using ML Techniques

To find the best standalone classifier for diabetes prediction, six different machine learning algorithms— RF, DT, KNN, AB, NB, and LoR—are used and compared across three diabetes datasets to identify the most effective standalone classifier for diabetes prediction.

5.1 Data Preprocessing

For the comparative analysis, three diabetes datasets (as mentioned in section 3.1) were used. All attributes with missing values were replaced with the mean of the respective columns. Next, we find how many attributes have numeric and categorical values as shown in table 5.1. Later, all the categorical attribute values are encoded into numerical values using LabelEncoder. Many ML algorithms perform better or converge faster when features are on a similar scale. For preprocessing operations such as scaling, it's very common to fit the model and then transform. So here we scale and normalize the data using Standard Scaler as mentioned below.

For each feature, *StandardScaler* transforms the data point X to X_{scaled} using the formula:

$$X_{scaled} = \frac{X-\mu}{\sigma} \qquad (5.1)$$

where:

μ is the mean of the feature in the training data.

σ is the standard deviation of the feature in the training data.

This transformation results in features having a mean of 0 and a standard deviation of 1.

Feature scaling by normalizing data boosted the algorithm's calculation.

Table 5.1. All datasets Attributes with the type of data

Datasets	Attributes with Numeric Data	Attributes with Categorical Data
Dataset 1	No. of Pregnancies, Glucose, BP, Skin Thickness, Insulin, BMI, Diabetes Pedigree Function, Age	Nil
Dataset 2	BMI, Sleep, Sound Sleep, Pregnancies	Age, Alcohol, BP Level, Family Diabetes, Gender, Junk Food, Prediabetes, high BP, Physically Active, Regular Medicine, Smoking, Stress, Urine Frequency
Dataset 3	Number of patient, age, urea, creatinine ratio, HbA1c, cholesterol, fasting lipid profile, TL, LDL, HDL, VLDL, BMI	Gender

5.2 Algorithmic Framework for Diabetes Prediction

To formalize the preprocessing and model evaluation framework described above, we present the algorithm for the Diabetes Prediction Pipeline as shown in Figure 5.1.

```
begin
  for each dataset in [Dataset1, Dataset2, Dataset3] do
     Replace Missing Values (dataset) ← mean (column_i)
     Identify Data Types (dataset) ← count (numeric, categorical)
     Encode Categorical Values (dataset) ← LabelEncoder (categorical_column_j)
    for each feature X in dataset do
        X_scaled ← (X − μ) / σ
    end for
     Split Data (dataset) ← 70% training, 30% testing
     for each model in [RF, NB, LoR, AB, DT, KNN] do
        TrainModel(model, training_data)
         EvaluateModel(model, test_data) ← accuracy, precision, recall, F1-score
     end for
      ConfusionMatrix ← compute(True Postive, True Negative, False Positive,
                                          False Negative)
  end for
  end
```

Figure 5.1: Diabetes Prediction Pipeline using ML models

This algorithm outlines the systematic steps applied across all three datasets, beginning with data cleaning and transformation, followed by feature scaling and normalization, and culminating in the training and evaluation of six ML classifiers. The inclusion of mathematical formulations (e.g., standardization, Bayes' theorem, sigmoid function, Euclidean distance, and Gini index) ensures clarity and reproducibility of the methodology. By presenting the workflow in algorithmic form, we provide a concise representation of the experimental design that underpins the subsequent comparative analysis.

5.3 Proposed Architecture for Diabetes Prediction

After completing essential data cleaning and preprocessing procedures, each dataset was partitioned to support fair and effective model development. For all three datasets used in this study, a randomized split was applied, allocating 70% of the data for training and the remaining 30% for testing. This commonly adopted ratio ensures that the models are trained on a sufficiently large sample while preserving an independent subset for evaluating generalization performance.

To assess the likelihood of diabetes occurrence, six ML classifiers (as discussed in section 4.1) were applied to each dataset: RF, NB, LoR, AB, DT, and KNN. These algorithms were chosen to represent a broad spectrum of classification approaches. ranging from probabilistic and linear models to ensemble and instance-based techniques.

Each model was trained independently on the respective training sets and evaluated on the corresponding test sets. This setup enabled a consistent comparison of algorithmic performance across different data sources. Accuracy scores were computed separately for training and testing phases to examine model fit and generalization. The comparison between these scores provided valuable insights into potential issues such as overfitting, underfitting, or dataset-specific variability. The architecture ensures consistency across datasets and provides a robust framework (as shown in Figure 5.2 for identifying the effective algorithmic approach to diabetes prediction.

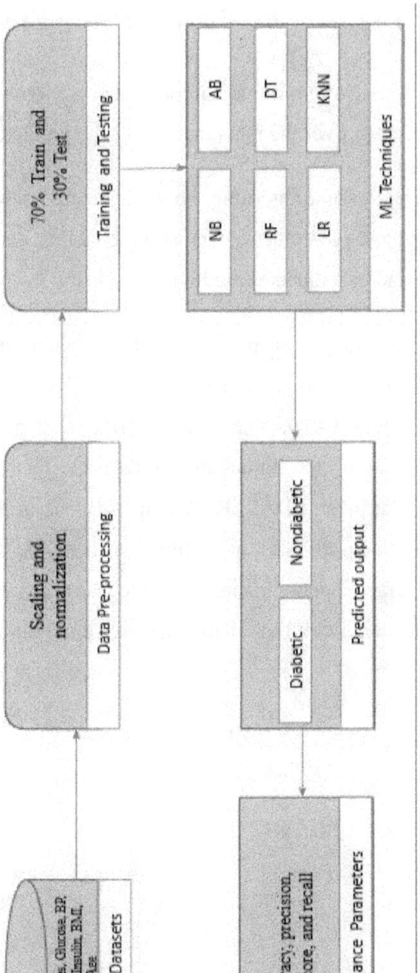

Figure 5.2: Diabetes Prediction model for different datasets

Model B: Diabetes Prediction Using Ensemble Classifiers

This method uses two ensemble approaches to combine several classifiers to improve prediction accuracy over the pima dataset for the prediction of diabetes.

From simple individual algorithms to sophisticated ensemble techniques, this model architecture permits systematic evaluation, enabling the identification of the strategy that produces the best diabetes prediction accuracy.

The goal of this study is to predict whether a patient has diabetes based on specific diagnostic measurements using ensemble classifiers, namely stacking and voting (as discussed in section 4.2). The study introduces a diabetes prediction model that applies preprocessing techniques to raw data and then employs ensemble classifiers composed of CatBoost, LDA, LR, RF, and GBC algorithms discussed in section 4.1. This model focused on a comprehensive methodology, which integrates preprocessing, model comparison, ensemble learning, interpretability, and deployment into a unified framework for reliable diabetes prediction, as shown in figure 5.3 and explained below:

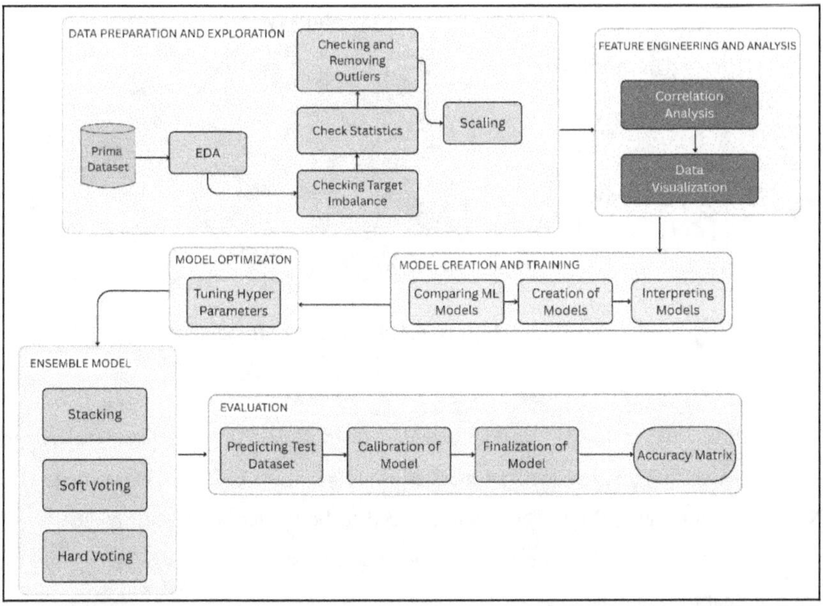

Figure 5.3: Architecture for Prediction of BGL using Ensemble Models

5.4 Exploratory Data Analysis

A raw Pima Indian Diabetes dataset is used here with 728 female records (as mentioned in section 3.1.1 for the prediction of diabetes), followed by preprocessing steps as mentioned below.

Data preprocessing is a crucial step in the field of ML, as it directly influences the model's ability to learn and the quality of insights obtained from the data. Therefore, it is essential to perform preprocessing before using the data in model development. The pie chart shown in figure 5.6 shows the proportion of diabetic and non-diabetic values in the 'Outcome' feature. The target is well balanced.

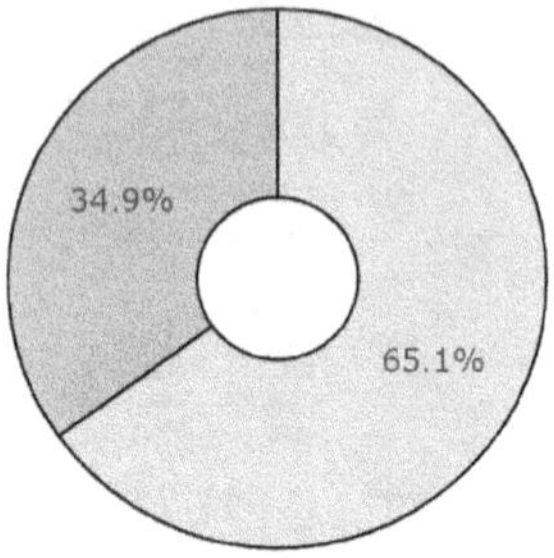

Figure 5.4: Pima Target Imbalance

From the statistics, we can see that from table 5.2 some features have minimum values of 0, which does not make sense (e.g., Glucose, BloodPressure, SkinThickness, Insulin, and BMI). These values need to be treated as missing values and imputed accordingly. Also, the standard deviation of some features is quite high, indicating that they may have outliers.

Table 5.2. Statistics for Pima Dataset

	Pregnancies	Glucose	BloodPressure	SkinThickness	Insulin	BMI	DPF	Age	Outcome
count	768.000000	768.000000	768.000000	768.000000	768.000000	768.000000	768.000000	768.000000	768.000000
mean	3.845052	120.894531	69.105469	20.536458	79.799479	31.992578	0.471876	33.240885	0.348958
std	3.369578	31.972618	19.355807	15.952218	115.244002	7.884160	0.331329	11.760232	0.476951
min	0.000000	0.000000	0.000000	0.000000	0.000000	0.000000	0.078000	21.000000	0.000000
25%	1.000000	99.000000	62.000000	0.000000	0.000000	27.300000	0.243750	24.000000	0.000000
50%	3.000000	117.000000	72.000000	23.000000	30.500000	32.000000	0.372500	29.000000	0.000000
75%	6.000000	140.250000	80.000000	32.000000	127.250000	36.600000	0.626250	41.000000	1.000000
max	17.000000	199.000000	122.000000	99.000000	846.000000	67.100000	2.420000	81.000000	1.000000

Although the zero values of each feature are converted to mean values, some features have a one-sided shape as shown in figure 5.5. Therefore, we decided to perform nonlinear scaling, and decided to use the QuantileTransformer that changes the distribution closest to the normal distribution.

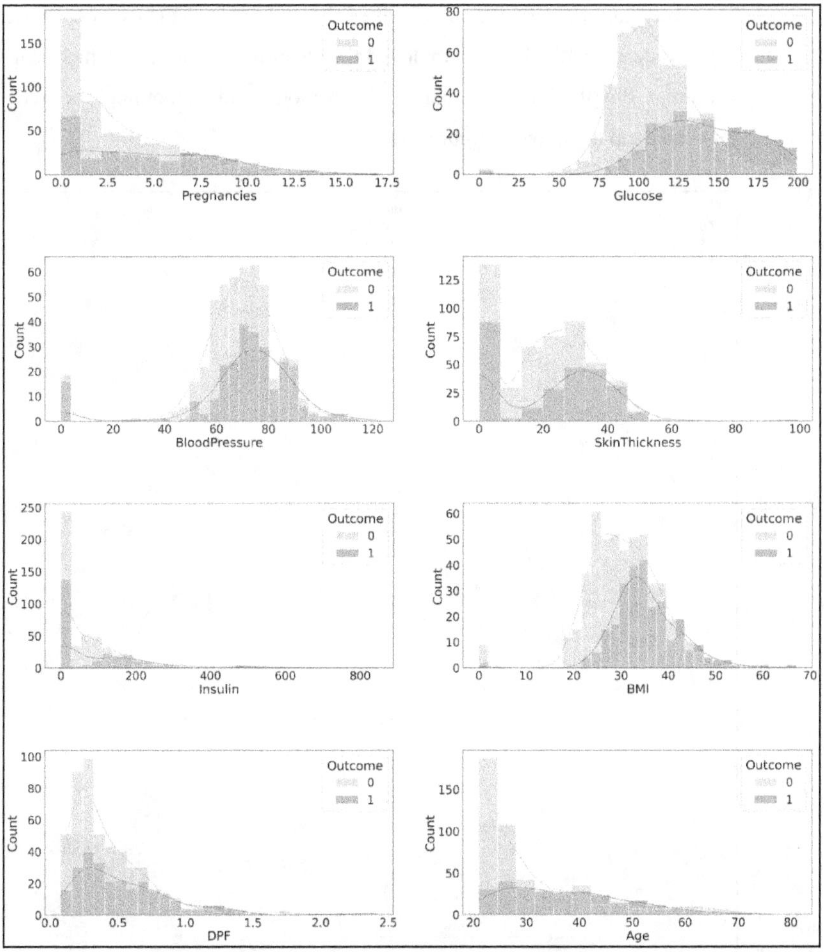

Figure 5.5: The distribution of features of Pima dataset

We observed that, high proportion of zero values was observed in the SkinThickness and Insulin features. When these zero entries were removed, the remaining data approximated a normal distribution. To address this, both linear scaling and standard scaling were initially applied. However, since replacing zeros with mean values still left some features with skewed distributions, nonlinear scaling was considered more appropriate. Specifically, we employed the QuantileTransformer, which maps data to a normal distribution by ranking observations and smoothing the relationships between them as shown in figure 5.6.

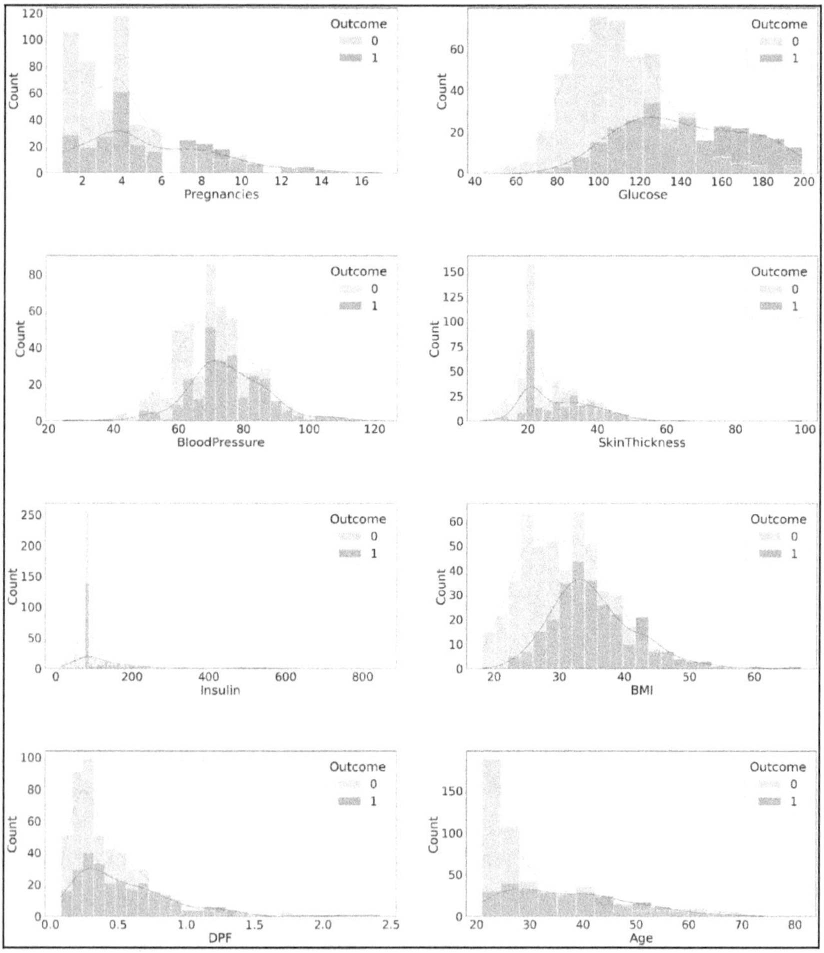

Figure 5.6: Histogram of the pima dataset

Looking at the picture above, you can see that the zero value is removed and scaling is done.

Correlation analysis, often referred to as bivariate analysis, is a statistical method used to assess the existence, strength, and direction of a relationship between two variables. It is particularly useful for rapid hypothesis evaluation and for guiding decisions on which variables warrant deeper investigation. However, it's important to note that even when a strong positive correlation is observed, it does not imply a causal relationship between the variables involved.

After scaling, feature selection was performed using a correlation-based approach to retain features with the strongest linear relationships, thereby enhancing model performance. The observations are drawn from figure 5.7, which shows feature correlation as:

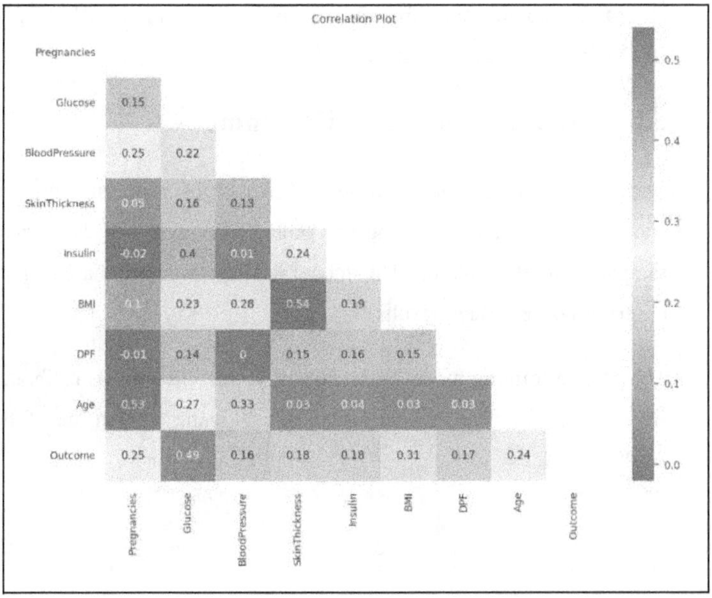

Figure 5.7: Correlation Analysis between variables

- Glucose shows a strong correlation with the outcome, indicating its significance in model training.
- BMI, age, and skin thickness have a moderate positive correlation with the outcome variable, which indicates that these features may be important predictors of diabetes.
- BMI has a moderate positive correlation with skin thickness, which may indicate that people with a higher BMI tend to have thicker skin.
- The highest correlation values are between BMI and skin thickness (0.54), age and pregnancies (0.53), and outcome and glucose (0.49).
- The other correlations are relatively weak or close to zero, such as insulin and pregnancies (-0.02) and dpf and pregnancies (-0.01).

The setup function was used to initialize the training environment and create the transformation pipeline. Using the built-in *compare_models*, various ML models were compared, and we found that the top five models, namely RF, LR, LDA, GBC, and CatBoost models, performed well.

5.5 Model Creation and Training

The model training process consists of two stages: processing the input data using a chosen method and comparing the generated output with the corresponding output sample from the dataset. The model is then adjusted based on the relationship observed between these results.

The best-performing model from the soft voting ensemble is calibrated using LoR to fine-tune probability estimates and then finalized with the full dataset using finalize_model.

5.6 Framework for Diabetes Prediction using Ensemble Models

To provide a systematic overview of the methodology, figure 5.8 summarizes the complete workflow for diabetes prediction using the Pima Indian dataset. The algorithm integrates dataset preparation, preprocessing (including handling of missing values, scaling, and feature engineering), exploratory data analysis, model training and comparison, hyperparameter tuning, ensemble methods, and finalization of the calibrated model. Each step is designed to ensure robust preprocessing, accurate classification, and interpretable results.

```
1: begin
2:   // --- Dataset Used ---
3:   Load Pima Indian Diabetes dataset (728 female records)
4:   Define target ← Outcome (binary: 0 = non-diabetic, 1 = diabetic)
5:   Define features ← {Pregnancies, Glucose, BloodPressure, SkinThickness, Insulin,
     BMI, Age, DiabetesPedigreeFunction}

6:   // --- Data Preparation and Exploration ---
7:   Identify invalid zero values in {Glucose, BloodPressure, SkinThickness, Insulin,
     BMI}
8:   Treat zeros as missing values → replace with mean(feature_i)
       mean(feature_i) = (1/n) Σ_{j=1}^{n} x_j
9:   Detect outliers using standard deviation thresholds
       z_score(x) = (x − μ) / σ
10:  Impute outliers with mean(feature_i)

11:  // --- Scaling and Transformation ---
12:  Apply StandardScaler:
       X_scaled = (X − μ) / σ
13:  If skewness persists → apply QuantileTransformer
14:  QuantileTransformer maps feature distributions → normal distribution
       Q(x) = Φ^{-1}(rank(x)/n)
     where Φ^{-1} = inverse CDF of standard normal distribution
15:  Confirm transformation by visualizing histograms and boxplots
```

```
// --- Exploratory Data Analysis (EDA) ---
Perform correlation analysis between features and Outcome
Pearson correlation coefficient:
r_{xy} = Σ (x_i − μ_x)(y_i − μ_y) / √[Σ(x_i − μ_x)^2 Σ(y_i − μ_y)^2]
Retain features with strongest correlations:
Glucose (r ≈ 0.49), BMI, Age, SkinThickness
Note feature relationships:
 BMI ↔ SkinThickness (r ≈ 0.54)
 Age ↔ Pregnancies (r ≈ 0.53)
Weak correlations: Insulin ↔ Pregnancies (r ≈ -0.02), DPF ↔ Pregnancies (r ≈
-0.01)

// --- Model Setup and Comparison ---
Initialize PyCaret classification environment (setup function)
Create transformation pipeline (scaling, encoding, imputation)
Compare multiple ML models using compare_models(metric=AUC)
AUC formula:
AUC = ∫_0^1 TPR(FPR) d(FPR)
where TPR = TP / (TP + FN), FPR = FP / (FP + TN)
Select top-performing models: RF, LoR, LDA, Gradient
Boosting (GBC), CatBoost

// --- Model Creation and Training ---
Train candidate models:
Logistic Regression (LoR):
      P(y=1|x) = 1 / (1 + e^{−(β₀ + β₁x₁ + ... + βₙxₙ)})
LDA (LDA):
      δ_k(x) = x^T Σ^{-1} μ_k − 0.5 μ_k^T Σ^{-1} μ_k + log π_k
Random Forest Classifier:
   RF prediction = majority_vote(T₁(x), T₂(x), ..., T_m(x))
Extra Trees Classifier
   CatBoost Classifier (gradient boosting with ordered boosting)
Gradient Boosting Classifier (GBC):
   F_m(x) = F_{m−1}(x) + η Σ h_m(x)
AdaBoost Classifier:
 F(x) = sign(Σ α_t h_t(x))
Evaluate models using cross-validation:
 Accuracy = (TP + TN) / (TP + TN + FP + FN)
 Precision = TP / (TP + FP)
 Recall = TP / (TP + FN)
 F1 = 2 × (Precision × Recall) / (Precision + Recall)
```

// --- Comparative Analysis of ML Models ---
Highlight CatBoost advantages:
Handles categorical + numerical features internally
Applies L1/L2 regularization:
$Loss = \Sigma L(y\_i, \hat{y}\_i) + \lambda_1 ||w||_1 + \lambda_2 ||w||_2^2$
Compare RF, LoR, CatBoost, LDA, GBC → CatBoost outperforms others (highest AUC)

// --- Model Interpretation ---
Apply SHAP values for feature importance
SHAP formula:
$\varphi\_i = \Sigma\_\{S \subseteq F \setminus \{i\}\} [(|S|! (|F|-|S|-1)! / |F|!) \times (f(S \cup \{i\}) - f(S))]$
Identify critical predictors:
Glucose (strongest), BMI, Age
SkinThickness → negligible contribution

// --- Hyperparameter Tuning ---
Use tune_model function for Top-5 models
Optimize parameters via 10 cross-validation folds
Select best-performing tuned models based on AUC and F1-score

// --- Ensemble Methods ---
Define Stacking Ensemble:
Base models ← {RF, LoR, CatBoost, LDA, GBC}
Meta-learner ← Logistic Regression
Define Voting Classifiers:
Soft Voting:
$\hat{y}\_final = \Sigma w\_i \cdot \hat{y}\_i$, *where* $\Sigma w\_i = 1$
Hard Voting:
$\hat{y}\_final = mode(\hat{y}_1, \hat{y}_2, ..., \hat{y}\_m)$

// --- Experimental Results ---
Evaluate ensemble models:
Soft Voting → superior predictive accuracy vs. Hard Voting
Calibrate best Soft Voting model using Logistic Regression
Finalize calibrated model using finalize_model on full dataset

// --- Finalized Model ---
Validate model with varying CV folds
Report final metrics (Accuracy, Precision, Recall, F1-score, AUC)
Confirm calibrated ensemble model outperforms individual classifiers
Conclude: Ensemble learning + calibration improves reliability of diabetes

prediction

69: ***return*** *the final calibrated ensemble model*
70: ***end***

Figure 5.8: Workflow for Diabetes Prediction using the Pima Indian Dataset

5.7 Comparative Analysis of ML models

CatBoost is a sophisticated version of gradient boosting; it has the capability to handle categorical and numerical data. Unlike other algorithms, there is no need for any external feature encoding methods, One-Hot Encoding or Label Encoding, since the algorithm handles categorical variables in an internal way. This algorithm works fine with regression and classification-type problems with more features. Also, it standardizes all the columns internally and does not require much data transformation. To prevent overfitting, L1 and L2 regularization methods are applied in CatBoost.

PyCaret is used for model building by setting up the classification environment and comparing several classifiers using AUC as the principal metric. Top-performing models selected include RF, LoR, CatBoost Classifier, LD), and GBC (GBC) based on the evaluation parameters shown in table 5.3. LoR models outperformed the remaining classifiers.

Table 5.3. ML model comparison for Diabetes Prediction

Models	Accuracy	AUC	Recall	Precision	F1	Kappa	MCC	TT (Sec)
LDA	0.7578	0.8306	0.5518	0.7007	0.6114	0.4407	0.4512	0.037
Logistic Regression	0.7615	0.8275	0.5623	0.7011	0.6192	0.4502	0.4591	1.247
Random Forest Classifier	0.7487	0.817	0.574	0.6717	0.6108	0.4291	0.4374	0.211
Extra Trees Classifier	0.7505	0.8148	0.5576	0.6794	0.6058	0.4277	0.4368	0.222
CatBoost Classifier	0.7448	0.8129	0.5678	0.6621	0.6064	0.4207	0.4266	2.539
Gradient Boosting Classifier	0.743	0.811	0.5944	0.6516	0.6167	0.4252	0.43	0.166
Ada Boost Classifier	0.7261	0.7871	0.5944	0.618	0.6019	0.3946	0.3978	0.115

5.8 Model Interpretations

Critical variables were examined in the training process using several classification algorithms to understand the behavior of the model. Model interpretation was done using SHAP values, which identified glucose, BMI, and age as the main predictors of the outcomes, while skin thickness had a negligible contribution to the training process. Figure 5.9 shows the feature importance results for the CatBoost and RF models.

The models are further optimized using hyperparameter tuning (tune_model) to enhance their generalization. This function is used to optimize the hyperparameters of a specified estimator. It generates a score grid containing cross-validation (CV) scores for each 10 fold, identifying the best-performing model based on the optimized parameters.The Top1, Top2, Top3, Top4, and Top5 models were tuned with different feature importance and decision boundaries.

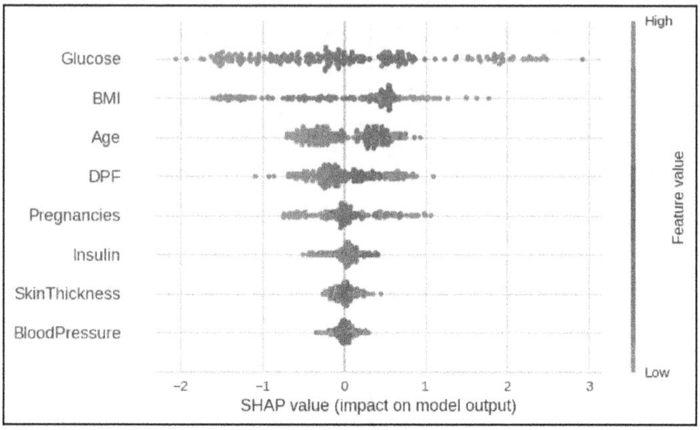

(a)

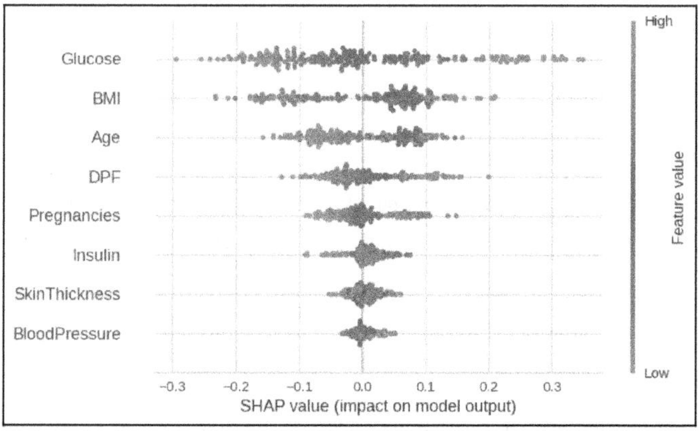

(b)

Figure 5.9: Interpretation of models (a) Catboost (b) RF

Model C: Prediction of Diabetes Blood Glucose Level

The third model of the project is dedicated to forecasting continuous BGLs, a more complex and dynamic regression problem. This model outlines a comprehensive methodology for analyzing diabetic patient data, predicting BGLs, and forecasting potential complications. The approach integrates data acquisition, preprocessing, augmentation, and the application of various ML and DL models. Our study employed a data-driven approach for blood glucose prediction and patient-specific clustering as mentioned below:

5.9 Data Preprocessing

For the prediction of BGL, the D1NAMO multimodal dataset is used here (as discussed in section 3.3). For all 9 diabetic patients, the data was captured for four days, i.e., from 1/10/2014 to 4/10/2014. The detailed tree structure of subject ID1, along with ECG, data generated from sensors, insulin, glucose, and food details, is represented in figure 5.10 and described in table 5.4.

```
diabetes_subset_ecg_data
|  └── diabetes_subset_ecg_data
|      ├── 001
|      |   └── sensor_data
|      |       ├── 2014_10_01-10_09_39
|      |       |   └── 2014_10_01-10_09_39_ECG.csv
|      |       ├── 2014_10_02-10_56_44
|      |       |   └── 2014_10_02-10_56_44_ECG.csv
|      |       ├── 2014_10_03-06_36_24
|      |       |   └── 2014_10_03-06_36_24_ECG.csv
|      |       └── 2014_10_04-06_34_57
|      |           └── 2014_10_04-06_34_57_ECG.csv


── diabetes_subset_sensor_data
|  └── diabetes_subset_sensor_data
```

```
|   ├── 001
|   |   └── sensor_data
|   |       ├── 2014_10_01-10_09_39
|   |       |   ├── 2014_10_01-10_09_39_Accel.csv
|   |       |   ├── 2014_10_01-10_09_39_BB.csv
|   |       |   ├── 2014_10_01-10_09_39_Breathing.csv
|   |       |   ├── 2014_10_01-10_09_39_RR.csv
|   |       |   └── 2014_10_01-10_09_39_Summary.csv


|   ├── 002
|   |   ├── food.csv
|   |   ├── food_pictures
|   |   |   ├── 001.jpg
|   |   |   ├── 002.jpg
|   |   |   ├── 003.jpg
|   |   |   ├── 004.jpg
|   |   |   ├── 005.jpg
|   |   |   ├── 006.jpg
|   |   |   ├── 007.jpg
|   |   |   └── 008.jpg
|   |   ├── glucose.csv
|   |   └── insulin.csv
```

Figure 5.10: Tree structure of data captured for Subject ID1

Table 5.4. Feature description of the D1NAMO dataset

Variable	Description	Type	Units
Glucose	CGM-measured blood glucose value	Time-series	mg/dL
Insulin	Insulin infusion rate	Time-series	U/min
CHO	Carbohydrate intake	Time-series	g

Physical Activity	Energy Expenditure	Time-series	Kcal/min
Heart Rate	Heart beats per minute	Time-series	bpm
Skin Temperature	Body temperature	Time-series	°C
Time	Timestamps (5-min intervals)	Sequential	—

5.10 Data Augmentation

A set of physiologically realistic data augmentation techniques was applied to generate one synthetic patient for each of the nine real patients. The CGM time series of each real patient was modified using controlled transformations that preserve underlying glucose dynamics while introducing natural inter-individual variability. These included a baseline shift of +5 to +12 mg/dL to mimic differences in fasting glucose levels and amplitude scaling (0.92–1.08) to simulate variations in glucose response strength. A circadian shift of up to ±90 minutes was used to account for differences in daily glucose–hormonal rhythms, while mealtime jitter (±10 minutes) reflected natural variability in eating patterns. Light Gaussian noise ($\sigma = 2$ mg/dL) was added to represent CGM sensor uncertainty. Additionally, post-meal peak timing and decay half-life were adjusted by ±8% to model variability in digestion, gastric emptying, and insulin action. Together, these augmentations generated realistic synthetic patient profiles that enhance dataset diversity and improve model generalization. Each newly generated augmented patient was subsequently assigned a unique identifier.

5.11 Framework for Blood Glucose Prediction and Diabetes Complication Classification

This algorithm, outlined in figure 5.11, is the complete pipeline used in the study, beginning with data preprocessing and feature engineering, followed by four modular DL architectures tailored to different patient cohorts and input modalities. Architecture 1 employs a DLSTM model with stacking and voting ensembles; Architecture 2 augments CGM data for small cohorts using CNN–LSTM; Architecture 3 scales CGM-only input using CNN–GRU; and Architecture 4 integrates multimodal physiological signals using LSTM–GRU hybrids. The framework includes evaluation across multiple forecast horizons using RMSE, MAE, MAPE, and MARD. Post-prediction, blood glucose values are clustered into six complication categories and classified using both SVM and RF models. Feature importance is computed using impurity-based ranking from the RF classifier to interpret the most influential predictors of complication risk.

```
begin
   Load D1NAMO dataset
   // --- Preprocessing ---
   Replace Missing Values (dataset) ← mean(column_i)
   Handle Outliers (dataset) ← replace with mean(attribute_i)
   Add Feature (dataset, "Calories")
   Combine Patient Data (dataset)
   Add Timestamp Index (dataset)
   Add PatientID (dataset)

   // --- Begin EDA and Feature Engineering ---
   Feature Engineering (dataset) ← {
      HR, RespRate, Activity, Acceleration, HR_confidence,
      DeviceTemp, CoreTemp, fast_insulin, type, Calories
   }
   Visualize Distributions (dataset) ← histograms, boxplots, correlation heatmaps
   Analyze Missingness (dataset) ← null counts, imputation strategy
   Encode Categorical Values(dataset) ← LabelEncoder
```

```
18:  Scale Features (dataset) ← StandardScaler
     X_scaled = (X − μ) / σ
19:  Normalize Target (BGL) ← MinMaxScaler
     X' = (X − X_min) / (X_max − X_min)
20:  Split Data (dataset) ← 80% training, 20% testing
21:  Temporal Split (dataset) ← reserve last 90 samples for evaluation

22:  // --- Architecture 1: DLSTM + Ensemble Methods ---
23:  Define DLSTM_Model:
24:     Input ← sequence [X_1, X_2, ..., X_n]
25:     LSTM_1 — 128 units + Dropout(0.2)
26:     LSTM_2 — 64 units + Dropout(0.2)
27:     LSTM_3 — 32 units + Dropout(0.2)
28:     Dense_1 — 16 units (ReLU)
29:     Dense_2 — 1 unit (Linear)
30:     Output ← BGL prediction
31:  Compile DLSTM_Model ← optimizer=Adam, loss=MSE
     MSE = (1/n) Σ (y_i − ŷ_i)²
32:  Train DLSTM_Model ← batch=32, epochs=10
33:  Define BaseModels ← [DLSTM_Model, LSTM–GRU, CNN–LSTM]
34:  StackingEnsemble ← Train meta-learner on predictions of BaseModels
35:  VotingEnsemble ← Weighted average of BaseModels' predictions
     ŷ_final = Σ w_i · ŷ_i, where Σ w_i = 1

36:  // --- Architecture 2: CGM Augmentation (9 → 20 Patients) ---
37:  Augment Patients ← generate synthetic CGM profiles
38:  Define CNN_LSTM_Model:
39:     Input ← sequence [X_1, X_2, ..., X_n]
40:     CNN_1D — 64 filters, kernel=3
41:     Max Pooling ← reduce temporal dimension
42:     LSTM ← 128 units
43:     Dense ← 1 unit
44:     Output ← BGL prediction
45:  Compile CNN_LSTM_Model ← optimizer=Adam, loss=MSE
46:  Train CNN_LSTM_Model ← batch=32, epochs=10
47:  EvaluateModels ← [DLSTM_Model, CNN_LSTM_Model, LSTM–GRU]

48:  // --- Architecture3: CGM-Only Scaling (20, 54, 100 Patients) ---
```

```
Define CNN_GRU_Model:
    Input ← sequence [X_1, X_2, ..., X_n]
    CNN1D — 64 filters, kernel=3
    Max Pooling ← reduce temporal dimension
    GRU ← 128 units
    Dense ← 1 unit
    Output ← BGL prediction
Compile CNN_GRU_Model ← optimizer=Adam, loss=MSE
Train CNN_GRU_Model ← batch=32, epochs=10
Evaluate Models ← [DLSTM_Model, CNN_LSTM_Model, LSTM–GRU,
CNN_GRU_Model]

// --- Architecture 4: Multimodal Input (50, 100, 426 Patients) ---
Define LSTM_GRU_Model:
    Input ← sequence [X_1, X_2, ..., X_n]
    GRU ← 64 units + Dropout
    LSTM ← 32 units + Dropout
    Dense ← 1 unit
    Output ← BGL prediction
Compile LSTM_GRU_Model ← optimizer=Adam, loss=MSE
Train LSTM_GRU_Model ← batch=32, epochs=10
Evaluate Models ← [LSTM_GRU_Model, CNN_LSTM_Model,
CNN_GRU_Model]

// --- Glucose Prediction Evaluation ---
Forecast Horizons ← {30, 60, 90 minutes}
Evaluate Model(model) ← RMSE, MAE, MAPE, MARD
    RMSE = √((1/n) Σ (y_i − ŷ_i)²)
    MAE  = (1/n) Σ |y_i − ŷ_i|
    MAPE = (100/n) Σ |(y_i − ŷ_i)/y_i|
    MARD = (100/n) Σ |(y_i − ŷ_i)/y_i|

// --- Diabetes Complication Classification ---
Cluster Predictions(BGL) ← categories [Hypoglycemia, Regular, Prediabetes,
Mild, Moderate, Severe Hyperglycemia]
Classify Complications_SVM ← train SVM on clustered BGL
SVM decision: f(x) = sign(Σ α_i y_i K(x_i, x) + b)
Classify Complications_RF ← train RF on clustered BGL
Evaluate Classifiers ← Accuracy, Precision, Recall, F1-score
```

```
// --- Feature Importance Analysis ---
Feature Importance_RF ← compute importance scores from trained RF model
    Importance (feature_i) = Σ (reduction in impurity from splits on feature_i)
end
```

Figure 5.11: BGL Prediction Pipeline using Ensemble and DL Architecture

5.12 Blood Glucose Prediction Models

For predicting BGL, we considered heart rate, breath rate, activity, acceleration, heart rate confidence, device temperature, CoreTemp, fast_insulin, slow_insulin, and type. Prior to model training, feature scaling and target normalization were performed using *StandardScaler* and *MinMaxScaler*, respectively.

The methodology for predicting BGLs leveraged both ensemble ML and DL models. For each patient, the augmented dataset was utilized for model training and valuation.

The glucose was designated as the target variable, with all other pertinent numerical features (excluding patient, level_0, and minute) constituting the input features. The dataset was partitioned into an 80% training set and a 20% testing set. Feature scaling was applied using *StandardScaler*, fitted on the training data and transforming both training and test sets. For all the models, a specific temporal splitting strategy was adopted where the last 90 minutes samples were reserved for evaluation, and the preceding data points were used for training The base models employed included a RF Regressor (RFR) a Gradient Boosting Regressor (GBR), and a Ridge Regression model. Two distinct ensemble methodologies were explored: a stacked regressor, where the predictions from the base models served as inputs to a final Ridge estimator, and a voting regressor, which aggregated predictions from the base models through averaging. Each of these ensemble models was rigorously trained on the prepared data, and their individual and combined predictions were generated to forecast glucose levels.

Model performance was quantitatively assessed using Root Mean Squared Error (RMSE) and Mean Absolute Relative Difference (MARD), with MARD being particularly relevant for glucose monitoring applications.

5.12.1 Architecture 1—BGL Prediction Without Augmentation

In this phase, models were trained directly on raw patient data without introducing synthetic samples.

The architecture of our proposed Continuous BGL model is illustrated in figure 5.12. The list of parameters considered for this experimentation includes CGM recordings generated after each 5-minute interval. All patients' data are combined by adding a timestamp as an index column and adding one more column of patient numbers. Missing values and outliers were replaced with mean values of the respective attribute. We consider three different types of neural networks, namely LSTM, GRU and hybrid model of LSTM and GRU to predict BGL. These models are defined by their architecture, specifically the number of layers and nodes per layer. To mitigate the vanishing gradient problem, we employed GRU and LSTM models. Furthermore, we optimized the models by exploring various hyper parameters, including the optimization algorithm, activation function, batch size, and learning rate. The BGL predictions were carried out for 3, 5 and 10 minutes of horizon. RMSE, MAE and MAPE metrics were used for evaluating performance of three models. Predicted glucose values are further categorized into diabetes symptoms (hypoglycemia, regular, prediabetes, Mild hyperglycemia, Moderate hyperglycemia and severe hyperglycemia) and its consequences using SVM discussed in table1. Finally, the SVM model performance is measured by evaluating accuracy, precision, recall, and F1-score.

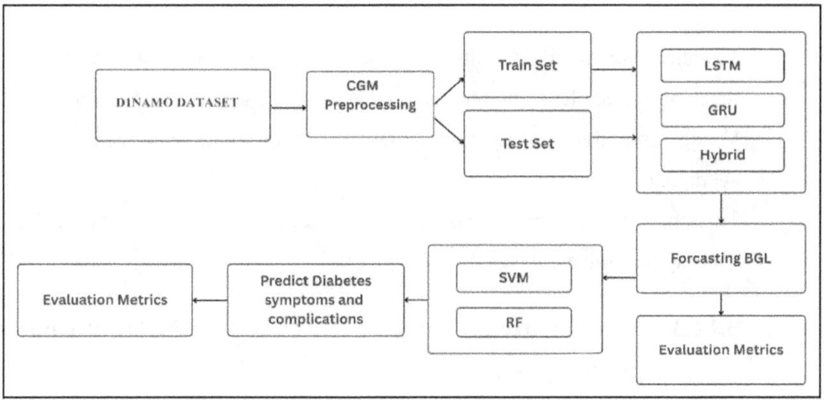

Figure 5.12: Proposed methodology for BGL Prediction

5.12.2 Architecture 2—CGM Experiments: 20 Patients → 20 Synthetic Patients

The BGL prediction experiments were conducted using progressively larger and more diverse datasets to evaluate model scalability, robustness, and generalization. This study leverages data from CGM and, in extended experiments, uses multimodal physiological and behavioral signals. Experiments are repeated with multiple patient cohort sizes and model architectures.

For the first experiment, the dataset contained 9 real patients, each contributing 4 days of CGM data. In using physiologically grounded augmentation techniques, one synthetic patient was generated from each real patient to form a total of 20 patient profiles. In this setting, only CGM glucose values were used as input features.

Models evaluated here are:

Deep LSTM (DLSTM)

LSTM–GRU hybrid network

CNN–LSTM hybrid architecture

To enhance predictive stability, two ensemble strategies were employed:
Stacking Ensemble: combining heterogeneous base learners using a meta-learner
Voting Ensemble: aggregating predictions from multiple models using weighted averaging.
This phase assessed baseline performance and inter-model consistency, using CGM as the only physiological signal.

5.12.3 Architecture 3—Scaling to Larger CGM-Only Cohorts (20, 54, and 100 Patients)

To assess model behavior for increasing cohort sizes, the same CGM input configuration was extended to datasets containing 20, 54, and 100 patients. The increase in dataset size now allowed for the evaluation of how model accuracy and error patterns evolved as inter-individual variability increased.
Models evaluated here are:
Deep LSTM (DLSTM)
LSTM–GRU
CNN–LSTM
CNN–GRU

The additional CNN–GRU hybrid was included in this stage as part of studying the differences in temporal–spatial feature extraction under broader patient diversity.

5.12.4 Architecture 4—Multimodal Physiological Input Experiments: 50, 100, and 426 Patients

A final, large-scale experimental series incorporated a richer set of physiological and contextual features beyond CGM. Datasets consisting of 50, 100, and 426 patients were used, each including heart rate, respiratory rate, physical activity level, acceleration, heart rate confidence index, device temperature, core temperature estimate, and patient type/metadata.

This multimodal configuration allowed the models to learn glucose dynamics driven by metabolic, behavioral, and therapeutic influences.

Models evaluated here are:
LSTM–GRU
CNN–LSTM
CNN–GRU

These architectures were selected for their complementary strengths in extracting local temporal patterns using CNNs and capturing long-range physiological dependencies using RNN-based units.

These configurations allowed for evaluating model scalability and performance consistency across different population sizes and data densities.

Figure 5.13 outlines a systematic pipeline for a complete BGL prediction model as described above.

The methodology for predicting BGLs leveraged both ensemble ML and DL models. For each patient, the augmented dataset was utilized for model training and evaluation.

This architecture is trained and evaluated using identical inputs and hyperparameters, allowing a fair comparison of their respective performance in predicting glucose levels over multiple forecasting intervals. It was conducted using the adam optimizer and mean squared error (MSE) as the loss function. This model was configured to forecast glucose levels at various future time points, aligning with prediction horizons like 30, 60, or 90 minutes.

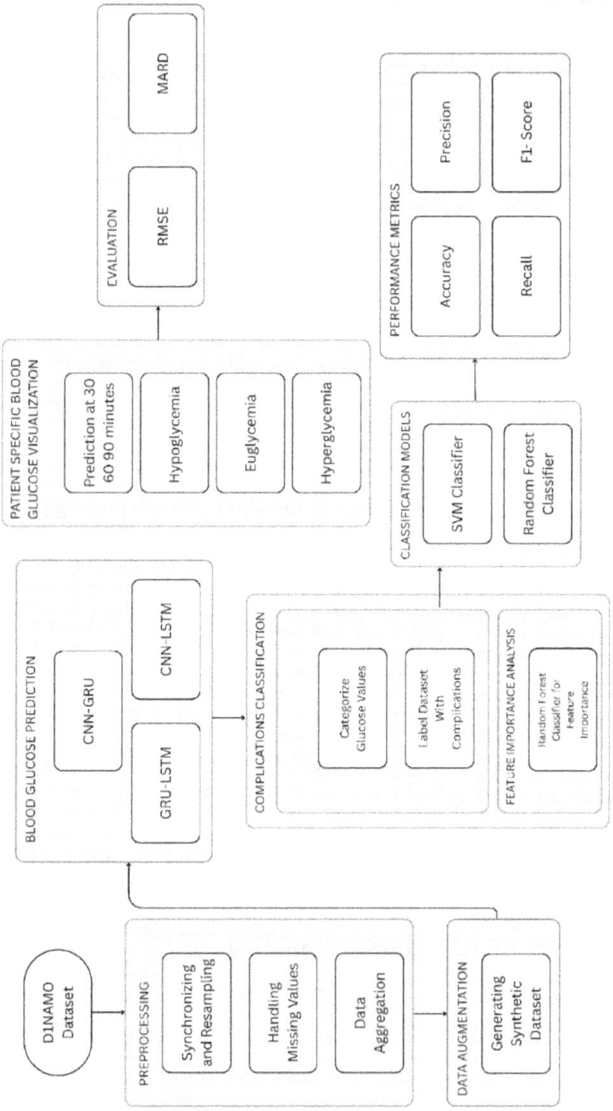

Figure 5.13: Proposed architecture for the Prediction of Blood Glucose Level

5.13 Model Architectures and Summary

This section discusses model architecture and summaries for each architecture:

5.13.1 Deep Long Short-Term Memory (DLSTM)

The first model employs a stacked LSTM architecture tailored for multivariate time-series prediction, particularly suited for glucose forecasting. It begins with an input sequence of physiological features, which is processed through three sequential LSTM layers with 128, 64, and 32 units, respectively. Each LSTM layer captures temporal dependencies at varying scales, enabling the model to learn both short-term fluctuations and long-term trends in glucose dynamics. Dropout layers with a rate of 0.2 are interleaved between the LSTM blocks to mitigate overfitting and improve generalization. The final LSTM output is passed through two fully connected layers: a dense layer with 16 units and ReLU activation, followed by a single-unit output layer that produces the predicted glucose value. As summarized in figure 5.14, the model comprises 132,001 trainable parameters, distributed across recurrent and dense layers. This architecture is effective for modeling sequential physiological signals and provides a strong baseline for comparison with hybrid models incorporating convolutional components. This model is particularly suited for capturing long-range dependencies and nonlinear dynamics inherent in physiological time series such as glucose levels.

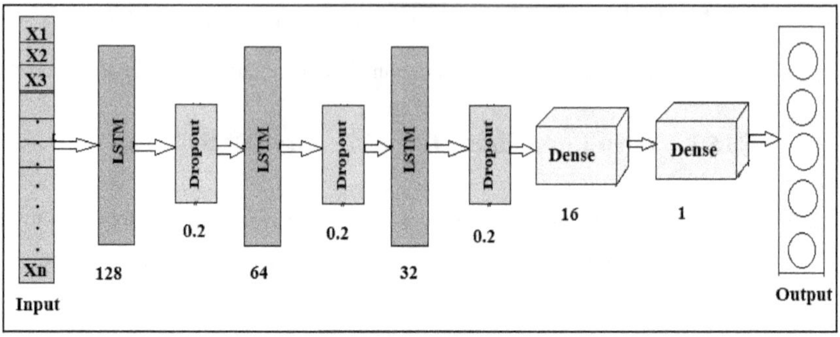

(a)

Model: "sequential"

Layer (type)	Output Shape	Param #
lstm (LSTM)	(None, 10, 128)	69,632
dropout (Dropout)	(None, 10, 128)	0
lstm_1 (LSTM)	(None, 10, 64)	49,408
dropout_1 (Dropout)	(None, 10, 64)	0
lstm_2 (LSTM)	(None, 32)	12,416
dropout_2 (Dropout)	(None, 32)	0
dense (Dense)	(None, 16)	528
dense_1 (Dense)	(None, 1)	17

Total params: 132,001 (515.63 KB)
Trainable params: 132,001 (515.63 KB)
Non-trainable params: 0 (0.00 B)

(b)

Figure 5.14: Architecture (a) and Summary (b) of DLSTM

5.13.2 Convolutional Neural Network-Long Short-Term Memory (CNN-LSTM)

The second model, the CNN-LSTM hybrid, leverages the strengths of convolutional and recurrent architectures. It begins with a 1D convolutional layer (64 filters, kernel size 3) that captures short-term patterns and local fluctuations in the multivariate input data. This is followed by a max pooling layer to reduce the temporal dimension and retain essential features. The output is then fed into a stack of two custom LSTM layers (64 and 32 units), each followed by a dropout for regularization, as shown in Figure 5.15. This combination enables the model to extract spatially localized patterns through the convolutional layer, while the subsequent LSTM layers capture sequential dependencies over longer time horizons. A dense layer with ReLU activation finalizes the prediction. The CNN-LSTM design is effective for inputs with strong local structure and periodic patterns, such as those seen in glucose sensor data.

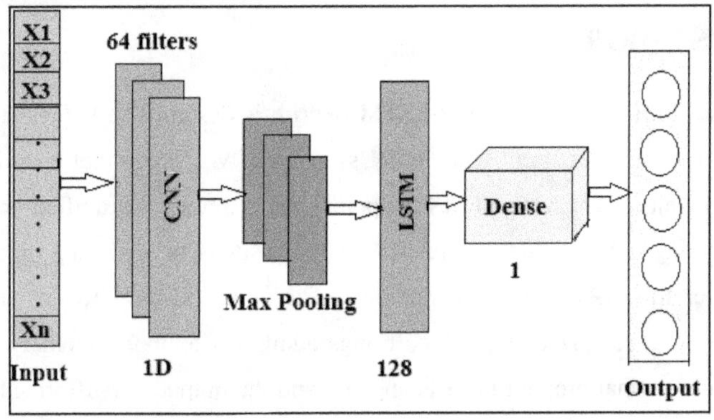

(a)

```
================================
Model: CNN + GRU
================================
Model: "sequential_3"
```

Layer (type)	Output Shape	Param #
conv1d_1 (Conv1D)	(None, 8, 64)	1,408
max_pooling1d_1 (MaxPooling1D)	(None, 4, 64)	0
gru_1 (GRU)	(None, 50)	17,400
dense_4 (Dense)	(None, 1)	51

```
Total params: 18,859 (73.67 KB)
Trainable params: 18,859 (73.67 KB)
Non-trainable params: 0 (0.00 B)
```

(b)

Figure 5.15: Architecture (a) and Summary (b) of CNN- LSTM

5.13.3 Long Short-Term Memory—Gated Recurrent Unit (LSTM-GRU)

The third model, the GRU-LSTM hybrid, is designed to harness the advantages of both Gated Recurrent Units (GRUs) and LSTMs. The initial layer is a custom GRU (64 units), which simplifies temporal gating through its unified update mechanism, offering computational efficiency and robustness to vanishing gradients. A dropout layer follows to mitigate overfitting. The output of the GRU is passed to a custom LSTM layer (32 units), which brings additional temporal memory depth via its cell state. A final dropout layer is applied, and the output is transformed via a dense layer with ReLU activation. This architecture shown in figure 5.16 allows the model to learn both fast-adapting short-term patterns (via GRUs) and persistent long-term patterns (via LSTMs), providing a balanced representation of the time series dynamics.

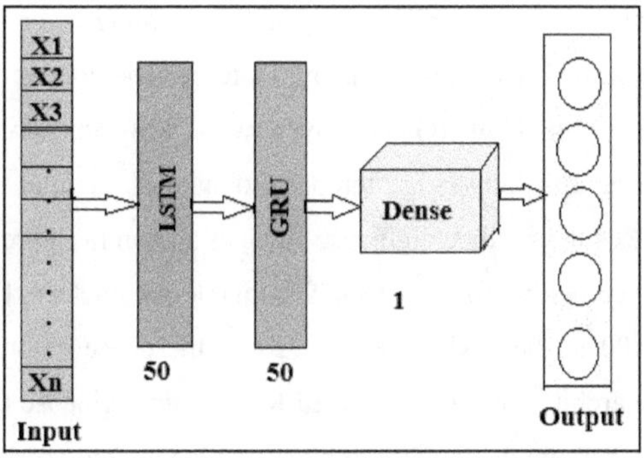

(a)

```
===============================
 Model: LSTM + GRU
===============================
Model: "sequential_1"
```

Layer (type)	Output Shape	Param #
lstm_3 (LSTM)	(None, 10, 50)	11,600
gru (GRU)	(None, 50)	15,300
dense_2 (Dense)	(None, 1)	51

```
Total params: 26,951 (105.28 KB)
Trainable params: 26,951 (105.28 KB)
Non-trainable params: 0 (0.00 B)
```

(b)

Figure 5.16: Architecture (a) and Summary (b) of LSTM- GRU model

5.13.4. Convolutional Neural Network-Gated Recurrent Unit (CNN-GRU)

The fourth architecture integrates convolutional and recurrent components to capture both spatial and temporal dependencies in physiological time-series data. It begins with a one-dimensional convolutional layer comprising 64 filters and a kernel size of 3, which extracts localized patterns and short-term fluctuations from the multivariate input sequence. This is followed by a max pooling layer that reduces the temporal resolution while preserving dominant features. The pooled output is then passed to a Gated Recurrent Unit (GRU) layer with 128 units, which models sequential dependencies and long-range temporal dynamics. A final dense layer with a single unit produces the predicted glucose value as shown in figure 5.17. The model consists of four layers with a total of 18,859 trainable parameters: 1,408 in the convolutional layer, 17,400 in the GRU layer, and 51 in the dense output layer. This compact yet expressive architecture is well-suited for real-time glucose forecasting, particularly in scenarios where input signals exhibit strong local structure and periodic behavior.

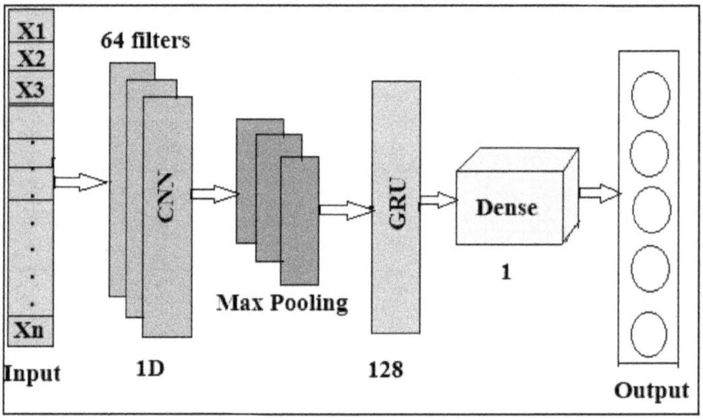

(a)

================================

Model: CNN + GRU

================================

Model: "sequential_3"

Layer (type)	Output Shape	Param #
conv1d_1 (Conv1D)	(None, 8, 64)	1,408
max_pooling1d_1 (MaxPooling1D)	(None, 4, 64)	0
gru_1 (GRU)	(None, 50)	17,400
dense_4 (Dense)	(None, 1)	51

Total params: 18,859 (73.67 KB)

Trainable params: 18,859 (73.67 KB)

Non-trainable params: 0 (0.00 B)

(b)

Figure 5.17: Architecture (a) and summary (b) of CNN-GRU

5.14 Training and Evaluation

All models were trained using the Adam optimizer and mean squared error (MSE) loss function for 10 epochs with a batch size of 32. The models were evaluated on the held-out test sequences (90 in total), and predictions were recorded for 30-minute, 60-minute, and 90-minute forecasting intervals. Two performance metrics were used:

Root Mean Squared Error (RMSE): Measures the absolute deviation between predicted and actual glucose values.

Mean Absolute Relative Difference (MARD): Measures the relative error, particularly critical in clinical glucose forecasting.

$$RMSE_{overall} = \sqrt{\frac{1}{N}\sum_{i=1}^{N}(y_i - \hat{y}_i)^2} \tag{5.14}$$

$$MARD_{overall} = \frac{100}{N}\sum_{i=1}^{N}\frac{y_i-\hat{y}_i}{y_i} \quad (5.15)$$

5.15 Patient-Specific Blood Glucose Clustering

In our framework for personalized diabetes management, an initial patient-specific clustering step is employed to categorize blood glucose readings based on established clinical guidelines. This process allows for a nuanced understanding of each individual's glycemic variability, moving beyond generalized population trends. Blood glucose values are categorized into distinct glycemic states as shown in table 5.6 along with their complications.

Table 5.5. Details of Diabetes Symptoms and Complications

Sr. No.	Diabetes Symptoms	Glucose Level Range (mmol/L)	Complications
1	Hypoglycemia 87, 88]	glucose_value<3.9	Confusion, dizziness, seizures
2	Regular [89]	3.9 <= glucose <= 5.5	No major Complications
3	Prediabetes	5.6 <= glucose <= 6.9	Risk of developing type 2 diabetes
4	Mild hyperglycemia [90, 91]	7.0 <= glucose <= 10.0	Early signs of neuropathy, risk of infections
5	Moderate Hyperglycemia [92, 93]	7.1<= glucose <= 13.9	Potential retinopathy, cardiovascular strain
6	Severe Hyperglycemia [94, 95, 96]	glucose_value>= 14	Diabetic Ketoacidosis (DKA), significant neuropathy, risk of nephropathy

These thresholds align with widely recognized clinical definitions for acute glycemic events and healthy blood glucose ranges, ensuring the clinical relevance of our clustering.

The following graph (Figure 5.18) represents a time-series plot of the true BG values for Patient 15 with the predictions made by the CNN-LSTM Model at different future horizons (30, 60, and 90 samples/minutes). Similarly the graphs with future horizons and analysis was conducted for all patients for all models.

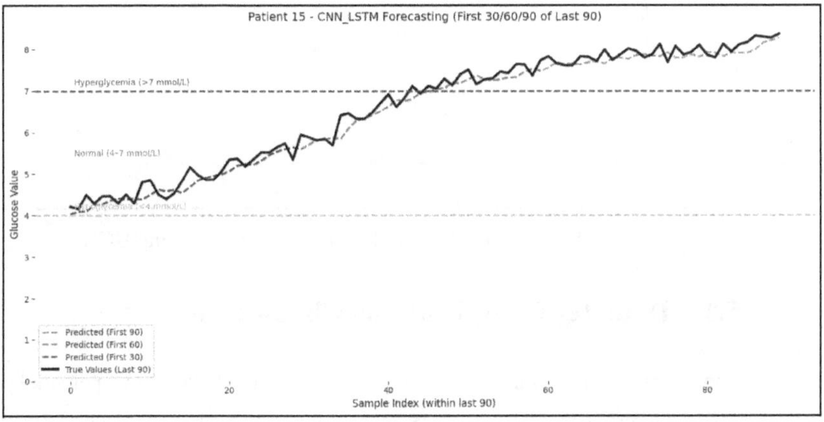

Figure 5.18: Blood Glucose Prediction for Subject 15 (pH= 30,60,90 Mins)

5.16 Feature Importance Analysis

To identify the most influential features contributing to diabetes complications, RF classifier was trained using physiological and behavioral attributes. Feature importance scores were extracted using the impurity-based ranking mechanism inherent to RF. As illustrated in Figure 5.19, the feature glucose emerged as the dominant predictor, followed by calories, posture, and heart rate. These insights highlight the critical role of glucose dynamics and metabolic indicators in forecasting diabetes-related complications.

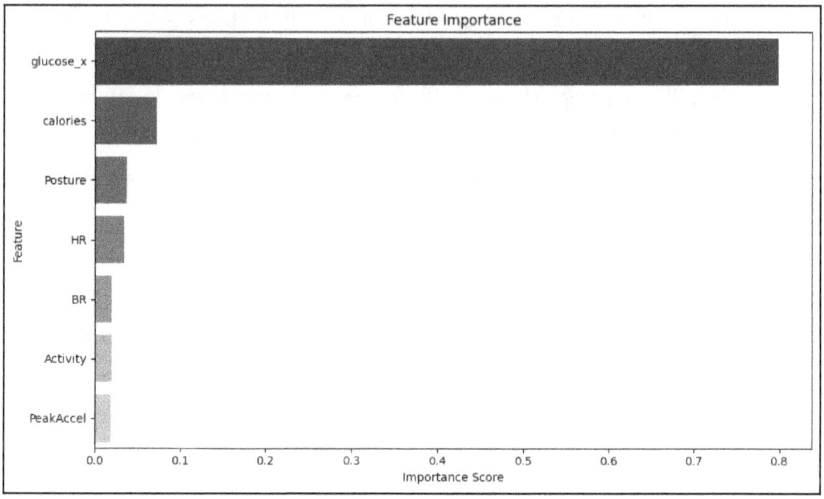

Figure 5.19: Feature Importance for Predicting BGL

5.17 Diabetes Complications Classification

The methodology further encompassed the prediction of potential diabetic complications based on glucose levels and other physiological parameters. To evaluate the ability of ML classifiers in identifying diabetes-related complications, both Support Vector Machine (SVM) and RF models were trained using physiological and behavioral features from the D1NAMO dataset. The complication categories included 'Hypoglycemia', 'Normal', 'Prediabetes', 'Mild Hyperglymia', 'Moderate Hyperglycemia', and 'Severe Hyperglycemia'. A specific subset of input features, comprising glucose, HR, BR, Activity, PeakAccel, HRConfidence, DeviceTemp, and CoreTemp, was selected for the classification task. Model performance was comprehensively assessed using standard classification metrics, including Accuracy, Precision, Recall, and F1-Score.

CHAPTER 6
RESULTS AND DISCUSSION

Model A: Comparative Analysis of Different Diabetes Datasets Using ML Techniques

6.1 Experimental Results

We found that ML models performed well on the following set of features when we trained models individually on these 3 diabetes datasets.

The accuracy of ML classifiers has been calculated by a confusion matrix. Figure 6.1 represents the arrangement of predicted and actual values in the confusion matrix. The result we got for the confusion matrix is represented in table 6.1.

Where,

0- Not Diabetic

1- Diabetic

TP- predicted result is diabetic and the actual result is also diabetic.

TN- predicted result is not diabetic and in actual result is also not diabetic.

FP- predicted result is diabetic but in actual the patient is not diabetic.

FN- predicted result is not diabetic and in actual it is diabetic.

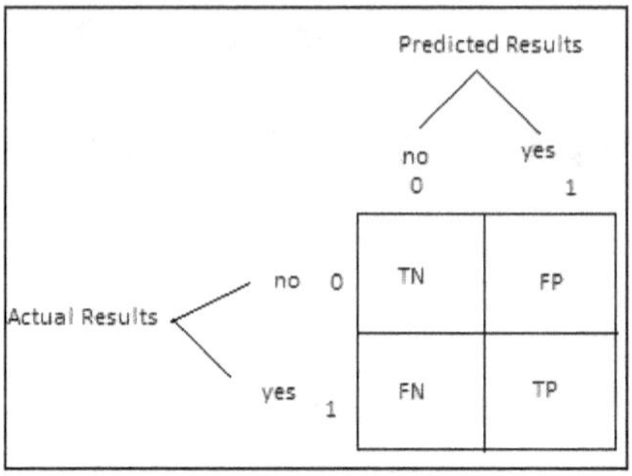

Figure 6.1. Confusion matrix for actual class vs predicted outcome

Table 6.1. Results of confusion matrix for NB, RF, LR, AB classifiers

Datasets		NB		RF		LR		AB		DT		KNN	
		0	1	0	1	0	1	0	1	0	1	0	1
Dataset 1	0	138	19	140	17	141	16	135	22	120	37	134	23
	1	36	38	34	40	35	39	36	38	26	48	30	44
Dataset 2	0	183	27	202	8	184	26	191	19	204	6	191	19
	1	20	56	8	68	22	54	12	64	8	68	16	60
Dataset 3	0	37	5	38	4	31	11	38	4	35	7	19	23
	1	15	243	5	253	7	251	16	242	2	256	14	244

The effectiveness of each ML model was assessed using key evaluation metrics, including accuracy, precision, recall, and F1-score. To ensure that the evaluation of these evaluation metrics is reliable and robust a 10 fold cross validation is performed. As illustrated in Figure 6.2 the accuracy results across all three datasets highlight RF as the top-performing algorithm, achieving 78% on dataset 1, 94% on dataset 2, and 97% on dataset 3.

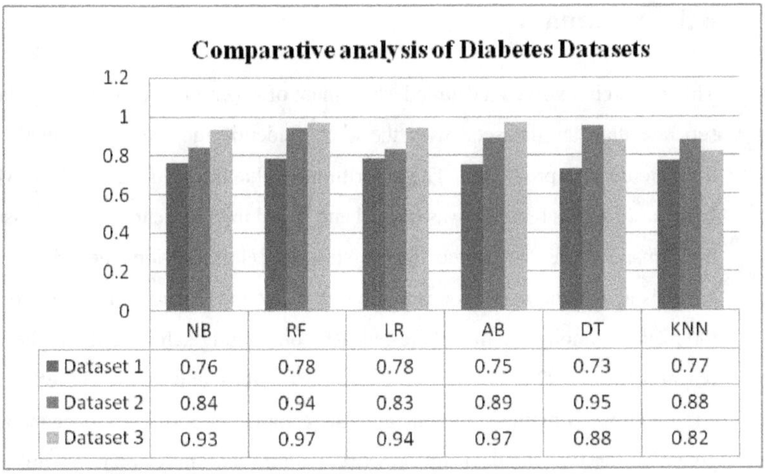

Figure 6.2. Accuracy of ML Models for Diabetes Prediction

6.2 Comparative analysis

A comparative analysis was conducted to evaluate the consistency of our results with prior studies that utilized Dataset 2 and Dataset 3. As outlined in Review 1.1., the findings reported by Neha Tigga [8] and Karlo Abnoosian [97] closely align with the outcomes of our experiments. Karlo Abnoosian employed an ensemble-based approach on Dataset 3 and achieved an accuracy of 96.80%, while our RF model produced a slightly higher accuracy of 97% on the same dataset. In the case of Dataset 2, the author applied a range of ML classifiers—including KNN, SVM, NB, DT, RF, and LoR —and reported an accuracy of 94.20%, which is comparable to the performance observed in our study. These comparisons reinforce the effectiveness of ensemble learning strategies in enhancing predictive accuracy for diabetes classification.

6.3 Summary

This research involved a detailed assessment of several ML classifiers applied to three separate diabetes datasets, with the aim of identifying the most reliable model for accurate disease prediction. The algorithms evaluated included KNN, SVM, NB, DT, LoR, and RF. Each model was trained and tested independently on all datasets, and its performance was measured using standard classification metrics. Comparative analysis across the datasets ensured consistency and helped validate the robustness of the results. Among the models tested, RF consistently achieved the highest accuracy, reaching up to 97% on Dataset 3. These findings underscore the effectiveness of ensemble-based methods in managing the complexity of medical data and affirm their potential for clinical decision support. Future work may focus on refining hybrid ensemble strategies to further improve predictive performance.

Model B: Diabetes Prediction Using Ensemble Classifiers

6.4. Experimental Results

This study employed three ensemble learning strategies to enhance the accuracy of diabetes prediction: stacking, soft voting, and hard voting. Stacking involved combining the outputs of five high-performing base models through a meta-classifier, while soft voting averaged the probability estimates from multiple classifiers. Hard voting, in contrast, determined the final prediction based on the majority class selected by individual models. Each ensemble method was evaluated using standard performance metrics, including accuracy, precision, recall, F1-score, ROC-AUC, and confusion matrix analysis.

Among the three approaches, soft voting demonstrated the most balanced performance, achieving high scores in both recall and precision. The stacking model, optimized using the area under the ROC curve (AUC), was constructed (as shown in

Figure 6.3) by integrating the top five classifiers (with accuracy LOR-76.15%, LDA-75.78%, ET-75.05%, RF-74.87% and catboost 74.48%). This meta-model was trained to learn from the probability outputs of the base models, enhancing its ability to generalize across varied feature combinations. Here LoR as top performing model selected as meta classifier. Figure 6.4 presents the confusion matrix for the stacking model applied to the Pima dataset, while the corresponding ROC curve indicates an AUC score of 0.85 for both diabetic and non-diabetic classes, reflecting strong classification capability.

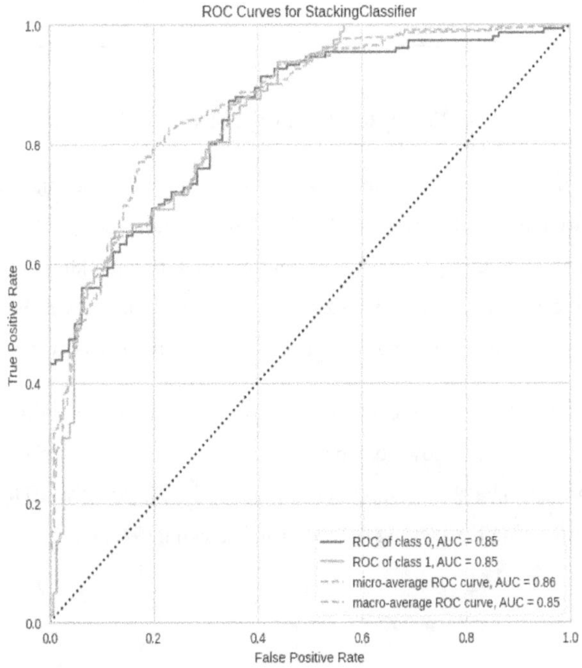

Figure 6.3. ROC curve for Pima using Stacking

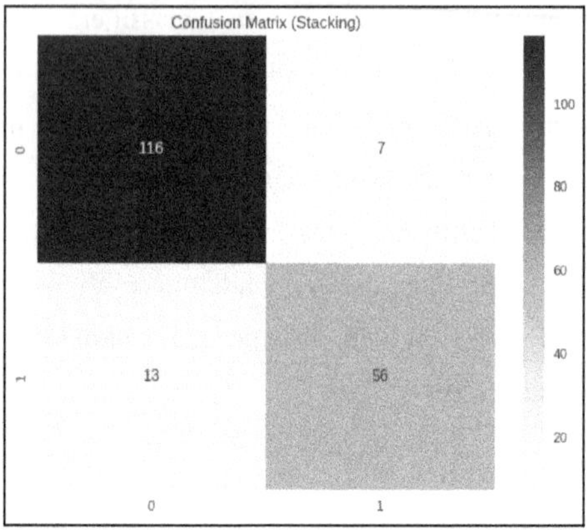

Figure 6.4. Confusion Matrix for Pima Stacking

In terms of overall accuracy, soft voting achieved the highest score at 92.71%, followed by hard voting at 91.15%, and stacking at 89.58%. To further improve predictive reliability, the best-performing soft voting model was calibrated using LoR, refining its probability estimates. This calibrated model was then finalized using the complete dataset, enabling both single-instance and batch-level predictions.

Figure 6.5 displays the confusion matrices for soft voting and hard voting classifiers, both of which show balanced classification across diabetic and non-diabetic categories. The soft voting model achieved the highest AUC score of 95.91%, outperforming hard voting (93.79%) and stacking (94.85%).

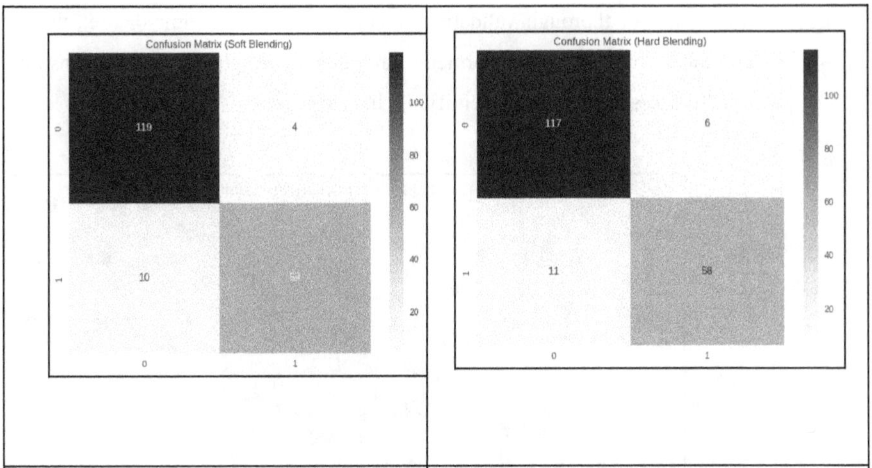

(a)	(b)

Figure 6.5. Confusion Matrix for a) Soft Voting b) Hard Voting

6.4.1. Calibrated Model

The experimental results indicate that soft voting offers superior predictive accuracy compared to hard voting. To leverage this advantage, the most effective soft voting model was selected and calibrated using LoR. This calibration step improved the reliability of probability estimates and enhanced overall model performance. The final calibrated model, trained on the full dataset, delivered the most consistent and accurate results among all ensemble techniques evaluated.

6.4.2 Finalized Model

The final model was refined by considering both the ensemble strategy and the number of cross-validation folds used during training. As shown in Figure 6.6, variations in fold count significantly influenced predictive accuracy, highlighting the importance of thorough validation. When applied to the Pima dataset, the calibrated ensemble model outperformed previous configurations, demonstrating its effectiveness in accurately identifying diabetes cases.

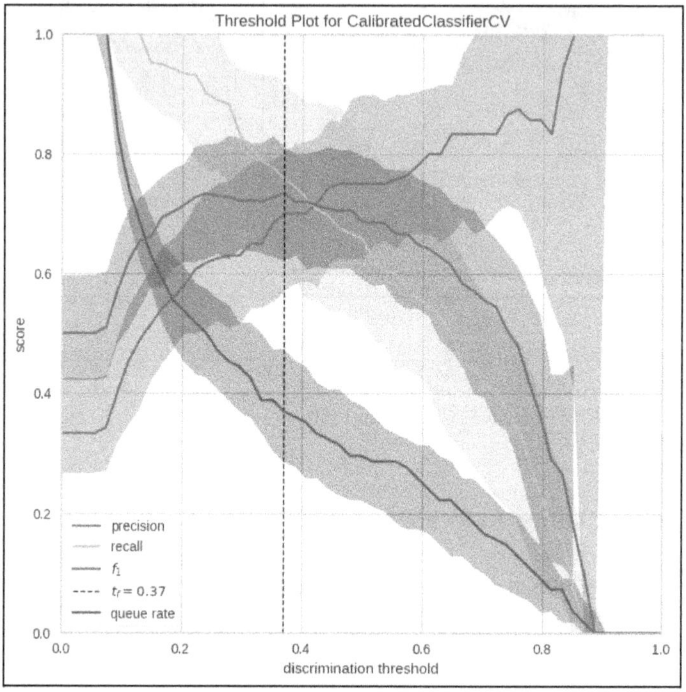

Figure 6.6. Threshold-based output

The performance of ensemble ML models for diabetes prediction was rigorously evaluated using accuracy, precision, recall, F1 score, and area under the curve (AUC) as performance metrics, as shown in figure 6.7.

Among the tested approaches, the Final Model yielded the highest accuracy (93.23%), precision (95.16%), F1 score (90.08%), and AUC (96.12%), demonstrating strong overall capability for distinguishing between diabetic and non-diabetic subjects. Soft Voting and Hard Voting ensemble methods also performed robustly, but with slightly lower precision and F1 scores. Notably, all models exhibited somewhat reduced recall values (ranging from 81.16% to 85.51%), indicating that a proportion of actual diabetic cases remained undetected. While high precision and AUC scores highlight the reliability of positive diabetes predictions, the lower recall underscores the need for further model adjustment to minimize the risk of missed diagnoses, which is especially important in clinical applications. These results position the Final Model as the most effective solution for accurate diabetes prediction in this study, but also indicate the value of future work focused on improving sensitivity for enhanced clinical safety and utility.

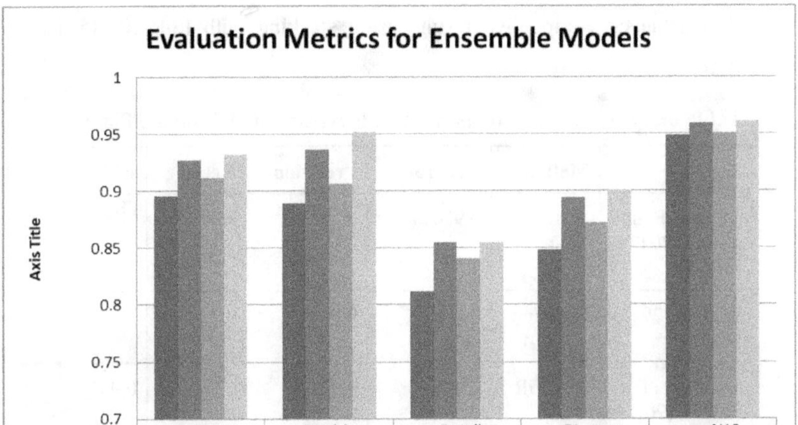

	Accuracy	Precision	Recall	F1 score	AUC
Stacking	0.8958	0.8889	0.8116	0.8485	0.9485
Soft Voting	0.9271	0.9365	0.8551	0.8939	0.9591
Hard Voting	0.9115	0.9062	0.8406	0.8722	0.9502
Final model	0.9323	0.9516	0.8551	0.9008	0.9612

Figure 6.7. Ensemble Models Comparison on Pima dataset

6.5 Comparison Analysis

Table 6.2 presents a comparative benchmark of ensemble machine learning methods applied to diabetes prediction using the PIMA dataset. The analysis evaluates multiple published approaches and the proposed model across key performance metrics: accuracy, precision, recall, F1 score, and AUC.

The Soft Voting method presented by Morgan-Benit et al. [85] reports the highest single accuracy at 0.9702, though it has limited metric coverage. Among comprehensively reported methods, the boosting approach by Li et al. [84] achieves 0.8884 accuracy with balanced precision (0.8432), recall (0.78), and AUC (0.95). The RFE-GRU strategy proposed by Shams et al. [96] demonstrates strong performance with precision, recall, and F1 scores all above 0.905, and AUC of 0.9278. Liu et al. [99] achieved competitive results using stacking with LoR (0.915 accuracy, 0.97 AUC).

Table 6.2. Performance comparison with existing studies on the Pima dataset

Authors	**Methods**	**Accuracy**	**Precision**	**Recall**	**F1 Score**	**AUC**
Morgan-Benit a et al. (2022) [85]	Soft Voting	0.9702	N/A	N/A	N/A	N/A
Li et al. (2023) [84]	Boosting	0.8884	0.8432	0.78	N/A	0.95
Shams et al. (2025) [96]	RFE-GR U	0.905	0.907	0.905	0.907	0.9278
Liu et al. (2025) [87]	Stacking+ LoR	0.915	~0.9150	~0.9150	~0.9150	0.97
Our results (2025)	Final Model	0.9323	0.9516	0.8551	0.9008	0.9612

Our model developed in this thesis surpasses existing methods with an accuracy of 0.9323, precision of 0.9516, recall of 0.8551, F1 score of 0.9008, and AUC of 0.9612. These results demonstrate superior overall performance, particularly in precision and balanced metrics, validating the effectiveness of the designed ensemble approach for diabetes prediction on the PIMA dataset.

6.6 Summary

This investigation demonstrated the potential of ensemble learning techniques in accurately predicting diabetes outcomes. Following exploratory data analysis and model selection, three ensemble configurations were developed and validated. Among these, soft and hard voting approaches proved to be the most dependable. The final model's performance was influenced by several factors, including classifier selection, preprocessing steps, and hyperparameter tuning. These elements may require adjustment when applied to different datasets or clinical scenarios.

The findings underscore the value of integrating ML with clinical data to support diagnostic decision-making. Future research should explore advanced ensemble architectures capable of capturing complex patterns and improving prediction accuracy across diverse medical datasets.

Model C: Prediction Of Diabetes Blood Glucose Level

This section employs results obtained from DL and hybrid architectures, both with and without data augmentation, to handle temporal dependencies and inter-patient variability. The systematic experimentation is performed by considering the following approaches shown in figure 6.8.

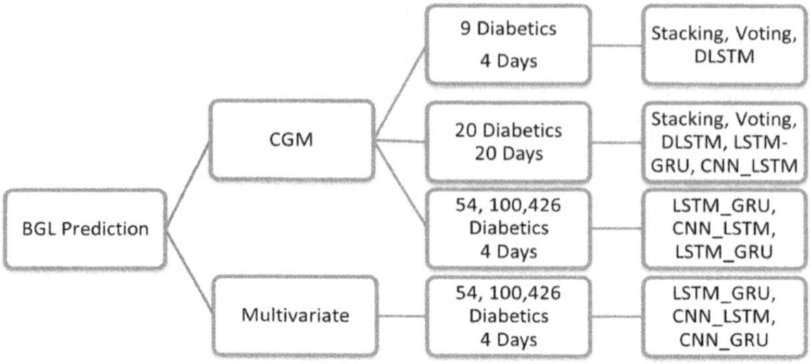

Figure 6.8. Systematic Approach for BGL Prediction Experimentations

Below is a detailed analysis of each result, followed by a comprehensive overall summary across all experiments.

6.7 Architecture 1 Results

This Model focused on short-term blood glucose forecasting using a highly constrained dataset consisting of CGM recordings from nine diabetic patients, expanded to twenty profiles through physiological data augmentation. Using only CGM input, the performance of DL and ensemble methods was evaluated to understand model behavior under minimal data availability. The results shown in figure 6.9 indicate that the DLSTM model significantly outperforms both stacking and voting ensembles, achieving an RMSE of 0.40 and a MARD of 3.73%. In contrast, the ensemble approaches demonstrate very high MARD values (22–25%), reflecting instability and overfitting due to limited data diversity. These observations confirm that purely recurrent deep models generalize more reliably than meta-learners when training data is scarce and establish DLSTM as the most suitable architecture for small CGM-only datasets.

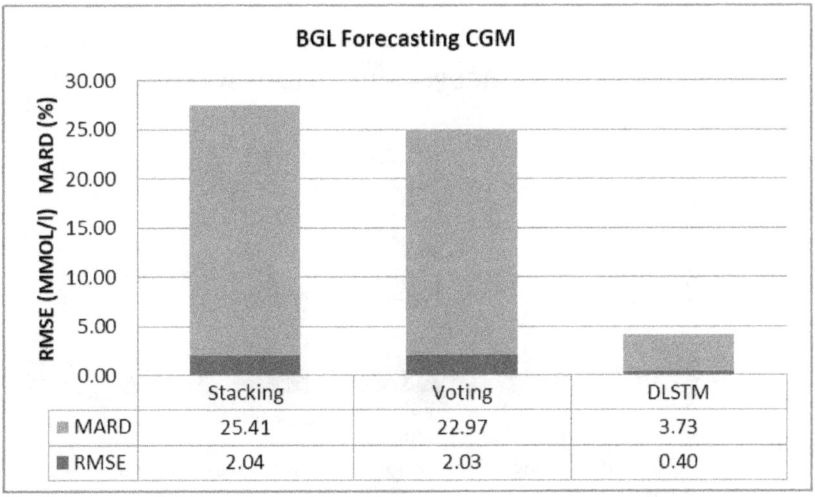

Figure 6.9: Results of BGL prediction for 9 diabetics

6.8 Architecture 2 Results

The chart (figure 6.10) displays performance metrics for five different models used to predict BGL for 20 patients. This progression enabled an examination of how increased inter-patient variability affects model robustness. The results represented above With 20 patients, stacking exhibited strong performance (MARD 2.799%), while the voting ensemble deteriorated sharply (MARD 16.126%), highlighting the sensitivity of unweighted averaging to outliers. As the dataset grew to 54 and 100 patients, hybrid architectures such as LSTM–GRU, CNN–LSTM, and CNN–GRU consistently improved in accuracy, while pure DLSTM became less dominant. The performance curves show a steady reduction in both RMSE and MARD as the cohort size increases, with CNN–LSTM and CNN–GRU attaining the most balanced and stable performance at 100 patients. These results demonstrate that hybrid CNN–RNN models scale effectively with dataset size and are better equipped to capture diverse glucose dynamics in moderately large populations.

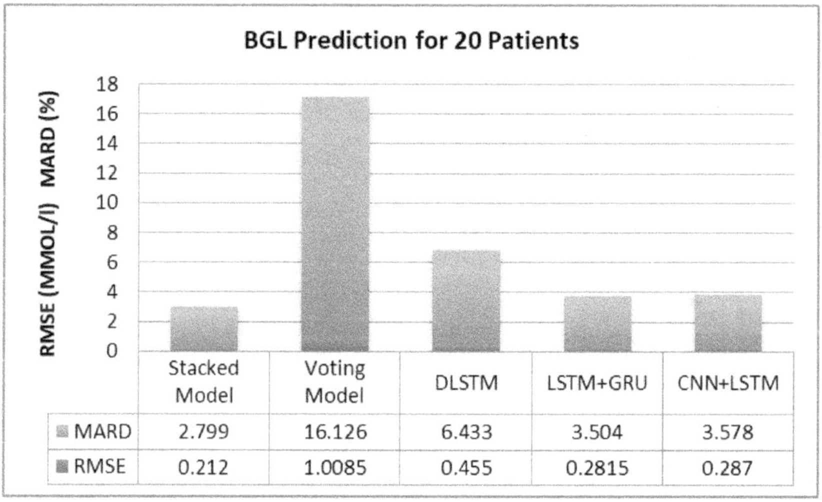

Figure 6.10: Results of BGL Prediction for 20 Diabetics

6.9 Architecture 3 Results

In this Model, the hybrid DL models were compared across large datasets involving 20, 54, and 100 patients. The results shown in figure 6.11 reveal pronounced improvements as the training population expands. CNN–LSTM and CNN–GRU networks consistently achieve lower RMSE values and reduced MARD percentages, reflecting their superior ability to extract both localized and long-range temporal features from CGM data. The LSTM–GRU architecture also benefits from increased sample diversity but remains slightly less stable than CNN-based hybrids. For the largest dataset (100 patients), the error metrics stabilize across all models, suggesting that around this cohort size, the networks capture sufficient inter-individual variability to generalize effectively. This Model establishes that hybrid CNN–RNN architectures are not only scalable but also consistently outperform pure recurrent models for large CGM datasets.

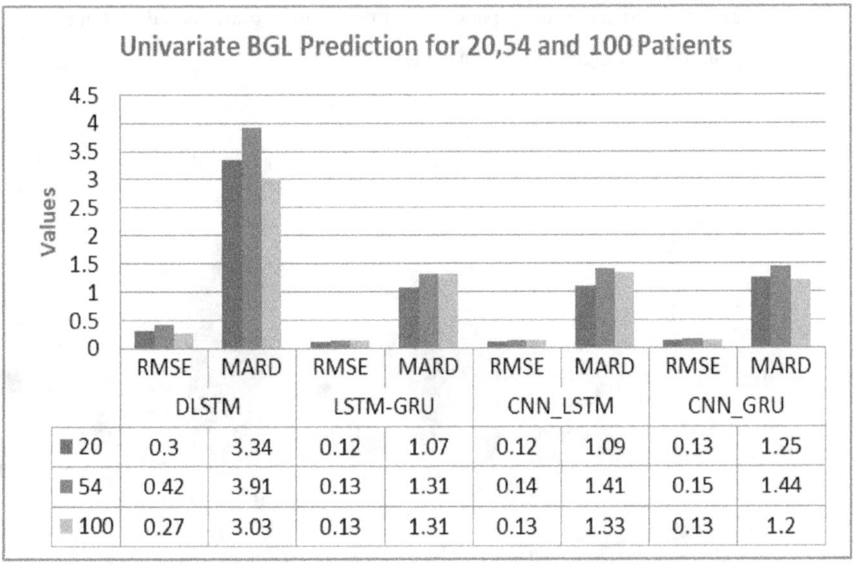

Figure 6.11: Results of BGL Prediction for 20, 54, 100 Diabetics

6.10 Architecture 4 Results

This Model incorporated multimodal physiological and behavioral signals, including heart rate, breathing rate, physical activity, accelerometer data, device and core temperatures, insulin dosages, and patient type. Using these rich input modalities across datasets of 54, 100, and 426 patients, all models exhibited notable performance gains compared to configurations as shown in figure 6.12. As dataset size increased, RMSE and MARD values consistently decreased, with the best results observed at 426 patients. CNN–LSTM achieved the highest accuracy (RMSE 0.12, MARD 1.02%), closely followed by CNN–GRU and LSTM–GRU. These findings underscore the value of multimodal physiological data in capturing the complex interplay of metabolic, behavioral, and treatment-related factors influencing glucose dynamics. The results also demonstrate that hybrid architectures leveraging convolutional layers extract meaningful patterns from multidimensional signals, enabling near–clinical-grade prediction accuracy.

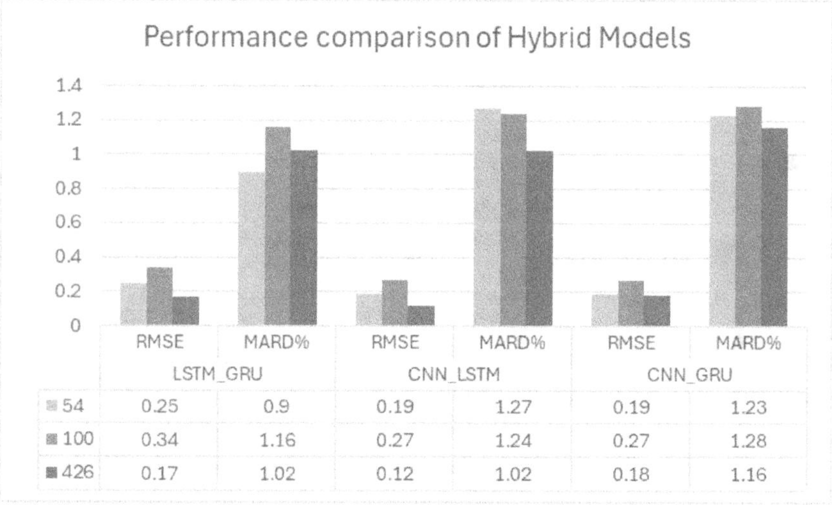

Figure 6.12: Results of Multivariate BGL Prediction for 54,100,426 Diabetics

6.11 Model Validation

Clarke Error Grid Analysis (CEGA) is used for visual assessment of the clinical accuracy of blood glucose prediction systems (CNN-LSTM Model) by plotting predicted vs. actual blood Glucose values on a different 5-zone grid as shown in table 6.3.

Table 6.3. CEGA Zones with respective Zone

Zones	Description	Obtained Results
Zone A (Clinically Accurate)	These values are within a 20% deviation of the reference value and are considered clinically correct.	38,246 predictions (99.75%)
Zone B (Benign Errors)	These values are outside the 20% deviation but do not lead to inappropriate treatment and are clinically acceptable.	45 predictions (0.12%)
Zone C (Overcorrect ion)	Values in this zone would lead to overcorrecting the glucose level, which can be risky.	37 predictions (0.10%)
Zone D (Failure to Detect)	This zone represents a significant failure to detect a clinically important high or low glucose level, which could delay necessary treatment.	Zone D: 0 predictions (0.00%)
Zone E (Erroneous)	These are the most dangerous errors, where the value could lead to performing the opposite of the required treatment.	12 predictions (0.03%)

The Clarke Error Grid Analysis (CEGA) for the CNN-LSTM blood glucose prediction model was performed on 426 patients, yielding a total of 38,340 prediction-reference glucose value pairs. The global Clarke Error Grid graph visually represents the distribution of these paired measurements across clinically defined zones (as shown in figure 6.13), providing insight into both the accuracy and clinical safety of the predictive model.

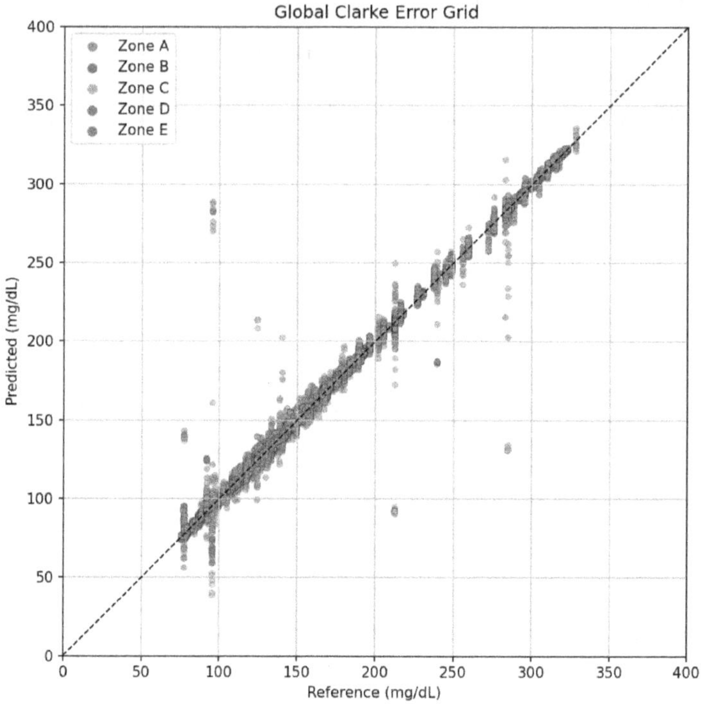

Figure 6.13: Result of Clarke Error Grid Analysis for 426 Diabetics

An overwhelming majority of prediction pairs are concentrated in Zone A, indicating that the CNN-LSTM model achieved clinically accurate results for nearly all samples.

6.12 Results of Diabetes Complication Classification

Model performance was comprehensively assessed using standard classification metrics, including Accuracy, Precision, Recall, and F1-Score, supplemented by a Classification Report and a confusion matrix to provide a detailed visualization of classification outcomes.

The RF model achieved near-perfect performance, with an overall accuracy of 99.99% and precision, recall, and F1-score values all exceeding 0.999 across all classes. In contrast, the SVM classifier also demonstrated strong performance, achieving an accuracy of 97.95% with balanced precision and recall values around 0.98 for each category. The results highlighted in table 6.4 shows the robustness of ensemble methods such as RF in clinical classification tasks, while validating the utility of SVM as a reliable alternative.

Table 6.4. Comparative Performance of RF and SVM Models for Diabetes Complication Classification

Metric	**Random Forest (RF)**	**Support Vector Machine (SVM)**
Accuracy	99.9975%	97.95%
Precision	99.9975%	97.61%
Recall	99.9975%	97.95%
F1-Score	99.9975%	97.94%

6.13 Comparative analysis

To contextualize the performance of our proposed CNN–LSTM model, a comparative analysis was conducted against existing studies employing ML techniques for blood glucose prediction. As summarized in Table 6.5, our model, trained on the D1NAMO dataset with 426 patients and a 90-minute prediction horizon, achieved an RMSE of 0.12 mmol/L (equivalent to 2.16 mg/dL) and a MARD of 10.02%. This performance surpasses that of Mohebbi et al. (2022) [11], who reported an RMSE of 11.74 mg/dL and MARD of 11.74% using a CNN–LSTM model on a private dataset with a 60-minute horizon. Similarly, Jaloli et al. (2021) [51] employed a stacked LSTM architecture on the DIAdivisor dataset (54 patients) and achieved an RMSE of 12.29 mg/dL and MAE of 10.31 mg/dL. Munoz-Organero et al. (2020) [100] used an

RNN–LSTM model on a smaller D1NAMO subset (9 patients), but did not report RMSE or MARD values. Notably, our model incorporated a richer set of input parameters—including CGM, heart rate, breath rate, posture, activity, peak acceleration, and calorie intake—which likely contributed to its superior predictive accuracy. These results demonstrate the effectiveness of multimodal physiological data and hybrid DL architectures in enhancing long-horizon glucose forecasting

Table 6.5. Comparative Performance of Blood Glucose Prediction Models

Author	**Dataset Used**	**PH (min.)**	**Input Parameters**	**Algorithm Used**	**RMSE** (mg/**dL)** **or (mmol/L)**	**MARD (%) or MAE (mg/dL)**
Mohebbi et al. (2022) [11]	Private	60	CGM, Insulin, Carb, Time-of-Day	CNN-LSTM	≈16.51 (mg/ dL)	≈11.74 (MAE)
Jaloli M. et al. (2025) [51]	DIAdvisor (54)	60	CGM	Stacked LSTM	13.79± 4.29 (mg/d L)	10.02±3.31 (MAE)
Munoz-Organero et al. (2020) [100]	D1NAMO (9)	60	CGM, Insulin, Food, Exercise	RNN-LSTM	<10.0 ((mg/dL)	Not Mentioned
Our Work	D1NAMO (426)	90	CGM, HR, BR, Posture, Activity, PeakAccel, calories	CNN_LSTM	0.12 mmol/L (equivalent to 2.16 mg/ dL)	1.02 (MARD)

6.14 Summary

Across all stages, the experiments systematically progressed from Small CGM-only datasets, Larger CGM-only cohorts, Large-scale multimodal physiological datasets,while evaluating a combination of recurrent, convolutional, and hybrid DL architectures as well as ensemble methods. This comprehensive design enabled assessment of performance trends as data complexity and patient variability increased.

This work has shown, throughout the four experimental Models, how dataset size, input richness, and model architecture are jointly influencing the accuracy of predictions of BGL. During the initial phase, having the CGM data of only nine patients, the variability was small, and hence poor performance resulted for ensemble techniques such as stacking and voting, while Deep LSTM was the only stable and accurate architecture. Subsequently, the dataset expanded to 20, 54, and 100 patients, and the reliability of the models showed great improvement: hybrid architectures, especially LSTM-GRU, CNN-LSTM, and CNN-GRU, started outperforming DLSTM. An increasing cohort size gave them sufficient diversity to better capture temporal glucose patterns, thereby reducing the prediction error. Meta-learners, like stacking, stabilized when moderate volumes of data were available, whereas voting remained sensitive to inconsistencies at the model level.

The integrated analysis across the four Models yields several important conclusions: first, model accuracy is strongly dependent on dataset size, with small datasets favoring simpler recurrent architectures and larger datasets allowing hybrid CNN–RNN models and ensemble methods to realize their fullest potential; second, hybrid architectures systematically outperform models that are purely recurrent when sufficient training data are available, especially for their increased ability to capture both local and long-range glucose dynamics; third, the incorporation of multi-modal physiological data provides the largest performance gains, by virtue of accounting for the complex interactions between metabolic, behavioral, and therapeutic factors that influence glucose variability; lastly, the top-performing configuration in all experiments presented in this work is the CNN–LSTM model trained on large multimodal patient cohorts, achieving low error rates suitable for practical diabetes management applications.

As the study progressed from large to large multimodal data, the advantages of a hybrid architecture became more pronounced. The CNN-based hybrids had consistent superior performance among the 20–100 patient datasets, reflecting their ability to describe the non-stationarity induced by both the short-term fluctuations and long-term dependencies in glucose signals. The greatest performance jumps came with the final Model, which incorporated the multi-modal physiological and behavioral features for the cohorts of 54, 100, and 426 patients. Variables like heart rate, breathing rate, activity, insulin dosage, and temperature provided important contextual information that was instrumental in improving modeling of glucose dynamics. With these enriched inputs, the CNN-LSTM and CNN-GRU models achieved near-clinical-grade accuracy with MARD values approaching 1%, thus demonstrating generalization across large and diverse populations.

Overall, the combined results clearly illustrate that the prediction performance increases with dataset size and multi-modal input complexity; similarly, the hybrid CNN-RNN models outperform the purely recurrent architectures when adequate data becomes available. The study concludes that the CNN-LSTM, trained on large-scale multimodal data, represents the most effective configuration for an accurate short-term glucose forecast, outlining its potential to become integrated within real-world diabetes monitoring and decision-support systems.

The CEGA confirms that the CNN-LSTM model achieves exceptional clinical accuracy, with 99.75% of predictions in Zone A and virtually no dangerous prediction errors. This performance strongly supports the model's reliability and clinical utility for blood glucose prediction.

CHAPTER 7

CONCLUSION AND FUTURE SCOPE

7.1 Conclusion

Diabetes mellitus is still one of the most important global health problems, and it needs accurate diagnostics and reliable forecasting of glucose to help with timely clinical decisions. This thesis brings forth a wide-ranging study that covers traditional ML, ensemble learning, and DL methods in advanced stages to improve predictions related to diabetes and forecasts regarding BGLs. The first part of the study involves a comparative evaluation among six ML classifiers on three different benchmark datasets related to diabetes. Results revealed that RF has always been able to achieve the best performance with accuracies going up to 97%, which indicates how strong an ensemble-based approach can be in medical classification tasks.

The second phase involves exploring ensemble learning approaches for the prediction of diabetes that leads to the creation of multiple ensembles with configurations like soft voting and hard voting. These models have shown good generalizability as well as stability across datasets; hence they are suitable for clinical decision support.

Based on insights gained from ML and ensemble methods, this research's last phase will focus on short-term blood glucose forecasting via DL. A multi-module framework comprising data preprocessing, feature engineering, model training, and performance evaluation has been developed using DLSTM, CNN–LSTM, LSTM–GRU, and CNN-GRU hybrid networks. Experiments carried out over 9 real diabetic patients as well as augmented real-patient CGM data along with multimodal physiological signals prove that the proposed CNN–LSTM model achieves highly accurate predictions, having an RMSE of around 2.16 mg/dL and a MARD of 1.02%, which outperforms contemporary approaches reported in literature.

The Clarke Error Grid Analysis shows that the CNN-LSTM model demonstrated clinically acceptable performance with the majority of predictions within zone A for glucose predictions, with only a minimal number of values in error zones that could impact treatment. This outcome substantiates the model's reliability and supports further deployment in personalized diabetes management—mirroring strong results reported in literature.

In general terms, this work contributes a unified framework for prediction of diabetes as a comparative multi-dataset evaluation of six ML classifiers for diabetes prediction, development of optimized ensemble strategies improving generalization and a design of a hybrid CNN-LSTM architecture for short term glucose forecasting using multimodal signals and clinical validation using clarke error grid analysis. In general, this thesis establishes a unified computational framework that integrates diagnosis and forecasting of blood glucose levels.. Findings from this study also highlight potential use cases for data-driven models toward improving early diagnosis supporting continuous monitoring plus enabling personalized management concerning diabetes.

The present study is constrained by the relatively small size of the original datasets, which were subsequently expanded through cohort synthesis and data augmentation. In addition, the predictive outcomes may have been influenced by sensor noise and inconsistencies arising from other health devices if used in real-time patient monitoring. Finally, validation on larger and more diverse real patient cohorts has not yet been performed, and such prospective evaluation will be essential.

7.2 Future scope

This research establishes a robust framework for diabetes prediction and complication classification, but future work should focus on validating the models with larger, multi-center datasets and deploying them in real-time healthcare applications. Incorporating explainable AI techniques and personalized medicine approaches will further enhance clinical trust and adaptability, while real-world trials will be essential to assess their impact on patient outcomes.

www.ingramcontent.com/pod-product-compliance
Lightning Source LLC
LaVergne TN
LVHW010733061126
851857LV00014B/1455